GREAT
MANAGERS
ARE ALWAYS
NICE

CHIP AVERWATER

Cover design by Ghislain Viau, Creative Publishing Book Design

ABB Press books are available through local and online retailers. Quantity discounts are available to organizations and associations. Custom editions and book excerpts are available as gifts and promotions. For more information please contact chip.averwater@gmail.com.

Printed in the United States of America
First Edition

ABB Press
www.abbpress.com
info@abbpress.com

Library of Congress Cataloging-in-Publication Data:
Averwater, Chip.
Great Managers Are Always Nice: Including Model Conversations/
Chip Averwater.
  p. cm.
  LCCN 2018930031
  ISBN-13: 9780983979005
  ISBN-10: 0983979006
  1. Management. I. Title.

Table of Contents

Introduction

You don't have to be a hard-ass to be a good manager. You don't need threats or discipline to get cooperation. You don't have to disown your friends to be their manager. You don't have to be a bully to get results.

You can be the nice person you are—and get better results. Your employees will work harder, enjoy their work more, stay at their jobs longer, appreciate your style, and respect your leadership.

This little book is not going to *tell* you how. It's going to *show* you.

We don't really learn to manage by reading about management—we learn by watching managers. Some inspire us and make work fun; some suck the motivation out of us and make us want to quit. From managers, good and bad, we learn how—and how not—to manage.

In this book we'll watch a legendary manager—Mike Mitchell of ABC Industries—as he handles all the challenging management situations. (No need to Google Mike or ABC—everything is right here.)

Mike, of course, gets extraordinary results; his team's products are among the most innovative, reliable, and respected in the world. And, as you might guess, he builds great teams; ABC's president, two vice presidents, and three division managers are former members of Mike's teams.

But the legend of Mike Mitchell stems from something else. It seems no one at ABC has ever heard Mike say an angry, disparaging, or offensive word to a team member. Ever! You see, Mike likes people—and, as often happens, people like Mike. As a manager, Mike is truly, and amazingly... well... *nice*!

We're going to follow Mike as he...

- welcomes a new team member (ch 7)

- makes his daily rounds (ch 8)

- conducts a team meeting (ch 9)

- delegates responsibilities (ch 10)

- coaches improvements (ch 11)

- corrects inappropriate behaviors (ch 12)

- counsels underperformance (ch 13)

- resolves disputes (ch 15)

- conducts performance reviews (ch 16)

- fires inappropriate team members (ch 17)

- helps his people advance (ch 18)

Yes, Mike is nice doing all these things. And, he makes it look easy.

Mike will be honored if you decide to copy his style—even his words, if you like. But, after you've seen him do it, you'll have the hang of it and can be nice in your own way.

Perhaps the legend of the nice manager in your company will be your own.

Chapter 1

Great Managers

A popular concept of an effective manager is a tough-talking, focused, no-nonsense taskmaster who makes and takes no excuses; he (or she) gets the job done.

Ironically, when people describe the best managers they've worked for, they say things like, "took time to explain things," "respected my abilities," "taught me a lot," "gave me opportunities to grow," "was willing to listen to my ideas," "supported me when...." This person sounds considerate, caring, helpful, and pleasant; we could call them "nice."

So which is really the good manager?

You're probably saying, "It depends on how you define 'good manager.'"

"If it's results you want, the no-nonsense manager is the one you're after; their singular focus and determination will get results."

"However, if you want a pleasant workplace where employees are happy and enjoy their work, you'll choose the more patient and supportive manager."

But do we have to choose? We want both. We need both!

Of course, we want results. Results are the reason our organizations exist.

But we also want a work environment that attracts good employees, inspires their best efforts, and encourages them to stay long term.

Can it be done? Can a manager be both results-oriented and nice?

It's not common, of course. But yes, it can be done.

It's what great managers do. They create a workplace where employees produce outstanding results, enjoy their work, and take pride in their achievements. Their people work hard and like their jobs (and their managers).

Great managers don't see themselves as practicing two conflicting types of management at once. On the contrary, they believe being nice is the key to achieving the extraordinary results their teams get.

They strive to be nice as often as possible. Their goal is to be nice in every situation. *Always* nice.

You probably find it hard to imagine how an effective manager can always be nice. Many people do. After all, every manager has to handle difficult situations occasionally—bad behavior, underperformance, breaking the rules, insubordination, even termination. "Sometimes a manager has to be firm—even tough," they say.

Indeed, a manager does face tough situations. And he can't shirk his responsibility to handle them. But that doesn't mean he can't be nice.

In fact, *every* situation can be handled nicely. And being nice always yields better long-term results than not being nice.

The measure of a manager is the situations he can handle with kindness and respect.

–Mike Mitchell

Almost all managers can be nice some of the time. Good managers can be nice most of the time. Great managers are nice all the time. *Always* nice.

In this book, we're going to see how legendary manager Mike Mitchell handles management situations—including, of course, the tough ones. Maybe you'll be surprised by how easy—and how much more effective—it is to be nice.

Maybe you'll even be inspired to try it yourself.

Chapter 2

Why Be Nice?

Great managers choose to be nice because nice...

Encourages Motivation: We know motivated employees produce more—in most cases, much more. They take pride in what they do, look for ways to do it faster and better, and work hard to achieve the goals they share with their teams.

Nice conveys respect and appreciation, keys to motivation. People enjoy doing things that are appreciated and they're respected for.

Improves Communication: Few employees feel they can be completely open with their managers. Consequently, many of the problems, challenges, mistakes, opinions, dissatisfactions, and plans of our employees are off-limits to us, their managers—despite being common knowledge to others in our companies.

Employees communicate more easily and more often with managers they're comfortable with. Nice opens the door.

Creates Confidence: An encouraging and supportive environment builds self-esteem, assurance, and confidence to perform, grow, and improve.

Employees who are afraid to make mistakes work slowly and don't try new methods or develop new skills. They don't reach their potential because they can't risk the consequences of failure.

> Confidence with enthusiasm is an unstoppable force; it accomplishes things we didn't consider possible.
>
> —Mike Mitchell

Attracts Better Employees: The best job applicants want more than a paycheck. They have multiple opportunities and can choose a job they feel they'll enjoy. They want to work where they feel welcome and appreciated.

Most make a point to find out about our work environment in their job interviews and from present employees, past employees, community reputation, and published reviews.

Increases Retention: Most people would rather stay where they're respected than take a chance on a new job, often even when they know they could earn more. Job satisfaction and enjoyment are high on their list of priorities; nice goes a long way in providing it.

> My goal is to teach them so well they could leave, but treat them so well they won't.
>
> —Mike Mitchell

Is Healthier: It's well documented that happy people are healthier, while stressed people develop hypertension, heart problems, high blood pressure—even colds, flu, cancer, and other diseases.

As managers, we can be the cause or the cure simply with the words we choose.

Is the Right Thing To Do: We're all human—we have similar challenges, desires, struggles, and goals. We can work together and make the best of our short ride together, or we can work against each other and make ourselves miserable.

Being nice is not more difficult, expensive, or inconvenient, but it can make a big difference in a day, a career, and sometimes a life.

Chapter 3

Always Nice?

Most managers can be pleasant when things are running smoothly, when everyone is doing their jobs, or when results are good.

But isn't it understandable to be frustrated by dumb mistakes, repeated errors, and poor results—especially if we really care about our work and goals?

Yes, of course. Occasional frustration is inherent in a manager's job.

But we don't have to show it!

"A word in anger is never forgotten" applies especially to managers. Our team members take our words seriously and remember them long after we've forgotten them. A moment of frustration and unguarded emotion can permanently scar a relationship. Nothing we say or do can take our words back or make up for them.

Even when our anger isn't directed at them, the scene is etched into their memories and reappears as a possibility in every interaction they have with us. They can never trust us not to do it again. We become like a potentially deadly bomb—regardless of how careful they may be not to set it off, the consequences of an explosion are too great to risk. So they keep their distance.

A manager who is always nice, however, teaches his people that they can trust him to respond calmly and respectfully. Team members are more comfortable interacting with him because they know what to expect.

They appreciate their manager's patience as they learn new skills, and they know their mistakes will be met with understanding. They recognize that their manager supports them and encourages their growth and improvement. And they're eager to help their manager and team achieve their goals.

> I hired you and I believe in you. Work with me and I'll help you succeed. Together we can accomplish great things.
>
> —Mike Mitchell

So why aren't more managers nice? Is it because...

...they've experienced authoritarian leadership from their teachers and managers?

...they've learned from their managers that a frustrating situation calls for a frustrated response?

...they feel their team members expect occasional unpleasantness from the manager?

...they're insecure in their authority and think it's helpful to show it occasionally?

...they believe an occasional display of unpleasantness proves their seriousness of purpose?

Or is it because they don't know how to be nice in every situation? They've simply never seen it done.

Chapter 4

You Can't Be Nice?

Some people say always being nice is unnecessary, a waste of time, or even impossible. Their arguments usually go something like this:

"I don't have time to be nice."

This is true for many managers. They have so many responsibilities and demands on their time that they can't worry about the work environment they create. They're fighting just to keep their heads above water.

Often, they point to their schedules and pressures as a badge of honor—a testament to their effort, value, and importance.

Perhaps they enjoy a fast-paced, high pressure, chaotic environment; some do. Most despise it. Certainly, it takes a heavy toll, both mentally and physically.

Too-busy-to-be-nice managers rarely build capable teams. Only people without other options are willing to work in an unfriendly environment, and they seldom offer their best efforts or stay long enough to become knowledgeable and helpful.

These managers could accomplish much more, as well as be happier and healthier, by stepping back temporarily, rearranging their duties, delegating some responsibilities, and developing a team to help them.

"This is a business, not a popularity contest."

Some managers (and companies) are so laser focused on results that they don't care about people and collateral damage.

What they miss is that we get better results when our employees are enthusiastic, enjoy their work, and stay at their jobs.

People are capable of ingenuity, determination, and extraordinary effort when they really want to achieve something. They do their best work when they feel respected, appreciated, and treated fairly. The little bit of time it takes to be nice pays big dividends in productivity, longevity, and happiness.

"I'm paying them! Now I have to be nice to them too?"

Paying someone only means they'll show up—probably. It doesn't mean they'll give their best effort, or even make a reasonable effort.

If they buy into what we're doing and feel like a respected member of the team, they'll do much better work than if they're just trying to qualify for the check. Perhaps they'll stay longer, too, saving us the time and expense of replacing them regularly.

"You don't know my employees."

Some employees are indeed contrary, unmotivated, or just plain lazy.

Sometimes they've learned their attitudes and behavior from difficult upbringings or life experiences. Often, they learn them from their jobs and their managers' expectations.

Some can be rehabilitated in an encouraging work environment. Many long for a manager who respects them and their abilities, and gives them a chance to show what they can do.

Others have problems that run too deep for us to fix. We can suggest changes and guide them toward help, but sometimes what they need is beyond our abilities, and we have to replace them.

> **We don't need people who will work for us; we need people who will work with us.**
>
> —Mike Mitchell

"You've got to remind them who's boss occasionally."

Does any employee ever really forget who's the boss? A manager's authority constantly looms over the workplace and all employees fear his disapproval.

A manager who reminds employees of his authority, even subtly, is resented. Employees hear what a manager says, even when they don't seem to. There's no need to add emphasis or pound the message home.

Managers who treat their people considerately and use their authority sparingly are respected and appreciated.

"Some people just don't respond unless you threaten them."

An employee with so little buy-in that only a threat motivates him isn't worth employing. He performs only when he's watched. He's minimally productive, frustrates motivated employees, serves as a bad example of what's acceptable, and drags down the attitudes and culture of the team.

Threats, scolding, and discipline are the worst of a manager's tools; they sap motivation and produce only temporary compliance.

If an employee with a poor attitude can't be swayed by polite discussion, he should be replaced with someone who shares the team's goals.

Encouraging words cost little but accomplish much.

–Mike Mitchell

"I try to be nice but some mistakes are just so stupid!"

Sometimes mistakes *are* hard to understand. And they're particularly frustrating when the consequences are significant.

But anger serves no useful purpose and is almost always counterproductive.

Regardless of how provoking a situation might be, it's always better to contain our frustration, think through the possible responses, and fashion a calm and considerate reply.

**"There's no way to be nice
when I have to reprimand or fire someone."**

Actually, it's not that hard. Later, we'll watch as our pro, Mike Mitchell, makes it look easy.

Chapter 5

Creed of a Great Manager

A great manager believes in his or her people—that they want to be part of the team, commit to a purpose, play a part, and help accomplish the team's goals. He knows there are some people who don't fit this description—but they're not on his team.

He sees his role not as an enforcer or disciplinarian but as a guide, facilitator, and coordinator. His focus is on communicating objectives, supplying feedback, developing skills, and recognizing and respecting efforts and successes.

> Treat people as if they are what you want them to become and they'll rarely disappoint you.
>
> —Mike Mitchell

He knows commitment is based on trust, and he works hard to build it. He never lies to his team members and is careful to deliver what he promises. He doesn't pretend to have all the answers; when he doesn't know, he says so.

He's comfortable admitting that his team members know their jobs better than he does and celebrates that as the strength of the team.

He often coaches behavioral changes but never with threats or discipline. He simply offers advice and recommendations and expects his people to respond positively.

He believes most people will live up to his expectations but realizes some cannot; they're distracted by personal problems, immaturity, psychological scars, substance abuse, and other challenges. He chooses his team carefully, and, when he makes a mistake, removes them as quickly (and as respectfully) as possible.

He wishes he could keep his best people forever, but he encourages them to expand their abilities and helps them advance in their careers. He takes pride in them and considers their success his success.

He believes practicing this creed not only helps the organization accomplish its goals—it enhances lives and makes the world a better place to live.

Chapter 6

Motivation

Motivation, perhaps the most important concept in management, is also the least understood. We know we want motivated employees, we know they accomplish more, and we know our organizations operate more smoothly with them. What we don't know is how to create motivation.

Despite hundreds of years of research to understand motivation and thousands of tomes to explain it, we still have no clear instructions for creating it.

Motivated people don't just get the work done; they find ways to do it faster and better.

Unmotivated people don't just do a little less; they never get started.

–Mike Mitchell

Rather than trying to make sense of complex academic theories, let's consider a simple analogy.

Think of a recreational sports team—adult basketball, for example. The players run and jump as long and as hard as their lungs and legs allow, fight for rebounds and loose balls, drench themselves in sweat, and exert themselves to the point of exhaustion. They yell, cheer, and exchange high fives, celebrate their wins, and mourn their losses.

Why?! They're paid nothing—often they pay to play. For their efforts, they get only sore muscles and dirty clothes. Yet they replay the games in their minds, relive their good and bad plays, practice to do better next time, and eagerly look forward to the next game.

Where does this extraordinary motivation come from?

The coach doesn't create it. He does little more than put the players in the game.

It comes from inside the players themselves—from the human instincts and social needs inside us all. The situation simply allows the players to express their natural inclinations.

The game lets the players...

- belong to a **T**eam;
- share **O**bjectives;
- **P**articipate in achieving them;
- see the **S**core;
- be **R**espected for their contributions & skills;
- **I**mprove themselves and their abilities.

The game is motivating because it meets these six powerful, innate, human needs. **TOPSRI**.

That's the kind of motivation we want in our companies and organizations. Why can't we get it?

We can! We can create a similar environment—an environment that lets our people express those same six needs.

It's what great managers do. Whether or not they recognize the acronym TOPSRI, they understand the six underlying needs, and they incorporate them into an environment that allows their people to express their innate motivation.

Chapter 7

A Motivational Environment

I don't create motivation–employees bring it. I only create an environment that encourages them to use it.

-Mike Mitchell

Let's watch for **TOPSRI** as manager Mike Mitchell meets with a new employee.

M: Welcome to our team, Frank.
As you saw from our hiring process, we're very careful in choosing who joins us. We're impressed with what we see in you, and believe you have the potential to be a star on our team.

Mike's use of "Team" indicates Frank's coworkers are committed to and working together toward a common purpose. By nature, people like belonging to a team—working with others, sharing objectives, proving their abilities, and being appreciated for their contributions.

His use of "we" instead of "I" implies respect for team members. He indicates it's an elite group, instilling pride in Frank for being chosen.

He conveys respect for Frank and expresses confidence in his abilities. Surely Frank would like to live up to those expectations.

And Mike lays out a challenge—for Frank to become a star. People enjoy challenges, especially when they involve proving skills and achieving valued objectives.

F: Thank you, Mr. Mitchell. I'll give it my best!

M: This morning, I'll give you an overview of what our team does and how we go about it.

We know we'll be the buyers' choice only if we make high quality, dependable products at reasonable costs. To judge how we're doing, we measure several things: our quality check scores, customer satisfaction ratings, costs per unit, and on-time delivery percentages. We set goals for ourselves for each of these, and we take pride in reaching them.

These are the **O**bjectives—the specific results the team strives for.

Notice that each objective is precise and measurable. "Produce high quality products" is not specific enough to be an effective objective; it's difficult to measure and would be subject to broad interpretations. Quantifiable objectives are clear, precise, and immediate indicators of performance, allowing the team to see and celebrate their accomplishments and focus on their shortcomings.

Objectives for other teams might include numbers of customers helped, invoices processed, response times, sales, products shipped, customer satisfaction scores, low error rates—measurements of whatever the team is trying to accomplish.

Objectives are motivational when they seem reasonable and attainable. Ideally, a team has significant influence in setting the objectives and, as a result, believes in and is committed to them.

M: You'll be in charge of purchasing parts and materials. You'll need to anticipate which materials manufacturing will need for its production schedule and coordinate with our suppliers to keep appropriate quantities. Your job is important to the team because if we run out of a part, manufacturing stops until we get it.

F: Sounds like a big responsibility.

M: [Smiles & nods] And that's why we were so careful in choosing you.

This is how Frank will **P**articipate.

Team members don't like sitting on the bench; they want to play a part, show what they can do, and be appreciated for their contributions.

Mike believes responsibility is an honor, not a burden, so he makes a point of telling Frank why his role is important to the team.

Playing a significant part inspires good team members to learn their jobs thoroughly and do them carefully. No one wants to let the team down.

M: Each day Lisa posts our numbers and any notable accomplishments. At our weekly team meetings, we get printed copies of the results and we discuss our successes, shortcomings, and potential improvements. Then we set our goals for the following week.

This is the Score. Good scores are a source of satisfaction; lesser scores point out problem areas and opportunities for improvement.

Discussing scores and goals in team meetings keeps them in focus, prompts thoughts on improvement, and encourages input and suggestions.

M: We like to celebrate our achievements.

F: I've heard.

M: At our weekly team meetings, we congratulate successful team members as well as take nominations and vote for an MVP.

If we reach our goals for the month we have a victory celebration—a catered lunch from a restaurant we vote on. During lunch, we announce outstanding contributions and give awards—they're just small tokens but team members take pride in how many they accumulate and display them proudly.

F: Looking forward to winning some awards.

Recognition of accomplishment, effort, and ability creates Respect. We like to do things we're respected for and, when we're respected, we work hard to do them better.

Opportunities to show respect are abundant—not just in team meetings and celebrations but in conversations, in introductions, by asking for opinions, deferring to judgments, giving credit, when assigning responsibilities, expressing interest, offering encouragement, or just by listening attentively when a team member speaks.

Respect costs only a little time and thought, yet yields extraordinary returns in attitude and effort.

F: I'm excited to play my part on the team, Mr. Mitchell, but I've got a lot to learn.

M: [Nodding] This afternoon, Sam, our director of manufacturing, will introduce you to some of our most experienced people and arrange for you to work alongside them. He'll also give you several of the company's training manuals; please take the certification tests as soon as you're ready.

F: Perfect.

M: You'll have continuing opportunities to expand your abilities, including training sessions, skill-sharing meetings, online modules, and company courses. There's also a library of training and self-improvement books and videos. And if you find an outside course you're interested in, we'll try to arrange it.

F: Great! I'm looking forward to all of that.

Training and education are opportunities to Improve—to enhance our abilities, increase our value, and advance our careers.

Getting an education is expensive; companies that provide it generously not only increase the effectiveness of their employees, they attract and retain more motivated people.

M: OK, any questions?

F: Only how soon can I get going?

A Note on Money as a Motivator

Some psychologists and researchers tell us money isn't a good motivator. They say businesses and organizations get better results by focusing instead on intrinsic motivation—personal satisfaction and enjoyment that comes from within us, as, for example, from a sense of purpose and an appreciation of the value of the work we do.

It is indeed motivating to believe what we do has value and importance—that we serve a larger purpose and, in our own way, make this world a better place. As managers, we can and should help our people understand and appreciate the value and importance of their work.

However, it seems dangerously misguiding to say that money is not an effective or appropriate motivator.

Most people, including especially high producers, readily admit to being motivated, at least in significant part, by money. And most business people recognize this. Almost all businesses encourage and reward with money—sales commissions, production bonuses, performance-based raises, profit sharing, year-end bonuses, stock options, and more. Indeed, it's nearly impossible to retain top talent without providing some measure of performance-based compensation.

Those uncomfortable with money as a motivator should remember that money represents our ability to take care of ourselves and our families—to provide a home, security, education, health care, etc., and to ensure we don't become a burden to society. Hopefully we're all motivated by that.

When monetary incentives are structured to reflect the value an employee creates for the company or organization, they are perhaps the fairest method of compensation.

Using money as an incentive and reward is in no way contrary to TOPSRI. To many people, money represents the Score—a measure of their effectiveness and the value they've provided.

Money also conveys **R**espect and recognition to family, friends, relations, and the public, who see what it buys as a sign of an effective and valued producer.

M: In addition to your salary, you'll get performance bonuses for maintaining appropriate inventory levels and avoiding production slowdowns.

The company also gives quarterly and annual bonuses based on how well the team meets its goals.

And, of course, raises and promotions are based on job performance. Each of these are meant to be recognition and appreciation of the work you do. They're an effort to share with you and your family some of the value you create for the company.

F: My family and I appreciate that.

If we want to attract and retain good people, we have to pay them fairly—and that means in proportion to the value they create.

Chapter 8

The Daily Rounds

Many of the duties of a manager are routine: keeping up with team members' activities, offering guidance, uncovering problems, providing help, and giving encouragement. An effective method of doing all these things is visiting regularly with each team member: the daily rounds.

Mike makes his rounds first thing each morning. In addition to getting his team started on time, it ensures that he helps his people with what they need before he gets buried in his own work.

Most visits are just casual updates—an opportunity to keep up with progress.

Making the Rounds
As work begins, Mike walks through the team's work area.

M: **Morning, Paul. How's it going?**
P: Great. I finished the Jackson project yesterday.
M: **Nice. Are you happy with it?**
P: I think they'll love it.
M: **[smile] What's next?**
P: I've got to work on... and....
M: **Anything you need?**

P: Just more time.

And on to the next person.

M: How ya doing, Cindy?
C: Good now. The new sorter arrived yesterday.
M: Does it do what you hoped?
C: Yeah, it's already saving me a lot of time.
M: Good. Everything else is OK?
C: As far as I know.

M: Hi, Ann. Catch me up.

But the visits are also a chance to make suggestions and provide guidance.

M: What's new, Frank?
F: Well, I'm trying to find a source for.... Seems the supply has dried up.
M: Who've you checked with?
F: All the regulars plus Allied gave me a couple of leads.
M: There was a guy in Sao Paulo who could turn up things like that. Sam knows who he is.
F: Thanks! I'll check with him right away.
M: Everything else OK?
F: That's my only challenge at this point.
M: Good luck.

And to offer encouragement and show appreciation.

M: Lisa, I got a note from Steve Thomas yesterday. He raved about how you solved his accounting issue. I'll make you a copy.

L: [smiling] Glad he's happy now.

M: After I read it at our team meeting, I'm going to send it upstairs to management.

Occasionally, they reveal someone is stuck or struggling and needs help.

M: Will, how's the new shipping software?

W: Terrible. I don't know why we had to change—the old software was fine.

M: [smile] Do you want me to see if IT can make sense of it?

W: It would be nice if someone could.

M: I'll give 'em a call.

Sometimes a few questions can uncover developing difficulties before they snowball into major problems.

M: Ann, I haven't seen an updated production schedule in a couple of days. Did I miss it?

A: No, I just haven't been able to get to it.

M: We really depend on that schedule. What do you need to catch up?

A: Just time. I'm getting interrupted constantly with things people need right away.

M: Sounds like we need to figure out something for that. Can we get together in about an hour?

Following visits are opportunities to check on progress and ensure the issue has been resolved.

M: **Is our idea for dealing with interruptions working?**
A: It's better. I'll give you the new production schedule in 20 minutes.

And occasionally a visit is a chance to make or adjust plans.

M: **Ben, I got word back from our Mexican distributor yesterday.**
B: Oh? Yes or no?
M: **Well, both I guess. They like the concept.**
B: But?
M: **They don't like the design.**
B: Wow! I put a lot of time into that design.
M: **And it looked good.**
B: What do they want?
M: **Don't know. What do you think about a conference call with Emilio?**
B: Good idea.
M: **I'll let you know when he's available.**

For employees who are offsite, a quick daily phone call can accomplish the purpose.

Only after Mike has checked with each of his people to ensure they have what they need to do their work, does he begin his own.

Chapter 9

Team Meetings

Employees are hired individually; as individuals, they'll show up, do the assigned work, and draw their pay.

When we organize them as a Team, they gain a sense of belonging and purpose that inspires a higher level of effort and participation. A team creates commitment to common goals and personal pride in their roles in achieving them.

The most effective setting for building and maintaining a team is team meetings. They allow members to share goals, coordinate roles and responsibilities, communicate progress, find opportunities for cooperation, participate in decisions, plan and adjust strategies, celebrate achievements, and more.

But meetings are time-consuming and expensive. Adding up the hourly costs of the attendees is often startling—the value of the work they might do in that time is presumably higher than that. As a result, team meetings need to be well planned, concise, and focused, and contain only information that is pertinent to everyone who attends. Topics and projects that don't involve the whole group should be discussed in smaller groups.

Attendees get the most from meetings when each has a responsibility and is encouraged to participate, collaborate, and share opinions.

Here's one of Mike's meetings:

Team Meeting
Tuesday morning, 8:30

M: Good morning. We're all here and on time. Thank you.

Starting on time shows **R**espect for the attendees and their time. Meetings that start haphazardly set an unfocused tone and indicate to team members it's OK to wander in—and sometimes out.

M: **Lisa distributed our team results. Lisa, can you summarize them?**
L: Our QC score this week was 99.2%, beating our goal by .2%. We had one return-for-quality—a problem with.... No safety incidents—3rd week running. We met our production schedule of.... And we....
M: **Results to be proud of. Congratulations!**

Putting results first on the agenda confirms the team's **O**bjectives and focus. The results tracked (preferably selected with input from the team) are the **S**core and send a strong message about the team's purpose and goals.

Delegating data collection and reporting to a team member creates **P**articipation in the meeting and signifies that the results are a team effort and accomplishment.

M: **MVP award. Gina?**
G: Nominations? Who did something extraordinary this week?
A: I'll nominate Frank. Our dealer in Des Moines needed an obsolete part for a key customer. Somehow Frank turned one up and shipped it overnight.
S: Ben. He devised a new fitting procedure that's faster and....

C: Rhonda. She....
G: Any more nominations? OK, all in favor of....
G: Rhonda is our MVP this week. [Applause as Rhonda accepts an MVP coffee cup.]

Weekly meetings are an ideal setting to recognize team members' contributions and to show and foster **Respect**.

Nominations from the team reflect and reinforce the team's values, and the team's vote enhances the award's value.

Awards need not be elaborate or expensive. The most treasured are often those that can be used proudly or displayed prominently—pens, cups, card holders, ribbons, certificates, etc.

M: Updates? Let's start with you, Karen, and go around the circle.
K: Last week we began the campaign for the new.... So far, we've got 83 orders. Now we're preparing for the Chicago show, and we....
M: Congratulations! Ben?
B: We finished the prototype for...; this week we'll get your feedback on it. Then we'll experiment with the finishes you've been asking for.
M: Looking forward to seeing both. Cindy?
C: On Friday we had....

Each person telling what they've accomplished since the last meeting and what they're working on now promotes teamwork, coordination, and understanding. People work together better when they understand each other.

M: Ok, sounds like a good last week and a full next week. Announcements?

K: There's a seminar Tuesday on.... Anyone who would like to attend can....

G: One of our dealers, Tom Walton of Armageddon, is in town and coming this afternoon for a tour. Please make him feel welcome.

M: **Thanks, Gina. Maybe we should straighten up our areas.**

A: Betty, in the main office, had her baby Monday if you'd like to send her a card or note.

T: She's a great resource for us. Why don't we send a group card?

M: **Good idea, Tom. Who can get the card and collect the signatures? Thank you, Rhonda.**

B: I'd like to get everyone's thoughts this week on our new....

M: **Any more announcements?**

And Mike dedicates part of each team meeting to **Im**proving knowledge and skills.

M: **OK, after Tom's amazing feat last week turning an unhappy customer into a big fan, I've asked him to share some of his magic with us this morning. Tom?**

T: ...

Speakers for team meetings are plentiful, but the best are often on the team. Many have accrued impressive knowledge and talent, and they've fine-tuned their skills and techniques to work in the specific environment.

A few minutes of each meeting spent on **I**mprovement add up to some impressive team skills. The topics selected reinforce the team's values and goals.

Inviting a staff member to share their knowledge conveys **R**espect. Most will work hard to prepare, examining and refining their ideas, planning their presentation, and enhancing their commitment to its concepts.

When needed knowledge doesn't already exist on the team, the topic can be assigned to a team member to research and present. The presenter typically works hard to make a credible presentation, becoming the team expert—another source of **R**espect, pride, and recognition.

M: Thanks, Tom. I picked up several ideas I'm going to use. We're out of time. Thanks to all of you for what you do. Let's have another great week.

Ending meetings on time again shows respect for team members and their time.

Mike's meetings are focused, positive, and participative. Humor and personal information and accomplishments are welcome in appropriate measure and enhance team spirit, but the conversation generally stays close to purpose.

A regular meeting schedule is the best assurance that the meetings will take place. Irregular and infrequent team meetings are difficult to schedule, as other priorities and obligations often preempt them until they're eventually abandoned.

Weekly is typically the right frequency and first thing in the morning tends to reduce conflicts and interruptions.

Team members who don't work onsite can attend by phone or video conference. Neither is as effective as face-to-face meetings, but they're often the best method available to help distant team members be part of the team.

Every team member should attend every full-team meeting whenever possible. Those who don't attend weaken their connection and coordination with the team, typically leading to misunderstandings, disagreements, and reduced support.

There are always a few team members who don't understand the value of building a team and feel their individual work should take precedence. When they skip a meeting, the rest of the team watches to see if it's allowed; if so, team meetings are soon sparsely attended.

Mike addresses absences quickly to prevent them from becoming habitual and spreading within the team.

Missing a Team Meeting
Mike finds Paul after Paul misses a team meeting.

M: We missed you in the meeting this morning, Paul. Is everything OK?

P: Yes, I just had to get ready for my customer this afternoon.

M: Is there a way to prepare before or after our meeting? You're an important part of the team and you often have something valuable to share. Plus, I like the others to hear what you're doing.

P: OK, I can do that. I didn't realize you needed me.

M: Thanks, Paul. I appreciate your positive attitude.

Small teams need meetings too. The excuse that, "We don't need meetings because we work so close together," doesn't hold water. Being close encourages coordination, but important topics like goals, assessing progress, recognizing contributions, and skills improvement are rarely covered outside a meeting format.

Small team meetings are usually easy to put together and can take place in a variety of locations.

A Small Team Meeting

*Gina, Karen, and Tom—the sales team—meet for breakfast
on Mondays. After the food is ordered:*

G: Shall we begin?

Gina's meetings are informal but follow a standard format that includes plenty of **TOPSRI**.

G: Here's the sales report through Friday. We made our target of....
K: Three weeks running.
T: We'd be way over if I could have gotten....

As a **T**eam, they set weekly sales **O**bjectives for the group.

G: Here are the individual totals for the month. Good numbers all around.
K: Mine aren't what I hoped for, but next week....

Individual numbers are each member's **P**articipation. No one wants to let the team down.

G: Tom, you're our sales leader so far this month. Congratulations.
K: But that won't stand long. [smile]

The sales report is the **S**core. Tracking and announcing sales leadership provides an opportunity to recognize team members and confer **R**espect.

G: **Updates. What are we working on?**
K: I'm getting closer to the sale to....
G: **Anything we can do to help with that?**
K: Actually, yes. They're asking.... Can either of you answer their questions about that?
G: **Tom, you're our expert.**
T: Sure, but you'll owe me, Karen. [smile]
G: **What else? Tom?**
T: I'm seeing Bob Taylor tomorrow and I'd like to show him the.... Do we have a sample?
K: [nodding] I'll give it to you after breakfast.
G: **I'm still working on the Mercer deal. Hopefully I'll close it Wednesday.**

In addition to promoting coordination and information exchange, the updates are a chance to hear and understand the challenges of fellow team members, make suggestions, get help, and find inspiration.

The sales team also uses the weekly meeting to make and adjust plans.

K: Have we made a decision about the Atlanta show?
G: **Not yet. What do you think?**
T: What were our totals last year?
K: 34k, I think.
T: I'd be in favor of skipping it and doing St. Louis instead.

G: Karen?
K: Yeah, let's give St. Louis a shot.
G: OK, I'll set it up.

Asking for and listening to the opinions of team members confers **R**espect; basing decisions on them confirms it.

G: Here's a list of in-stock inventory and the production schedule. Also, the M-12 is now discontinued. Here are the specs on the replacement.
T: I've had a couple of inquiries about the new.... Either of you know about it?
K: Not really.
G: Should I invite Ben to tell us about it at next week's breakfast?
K: It would help me.

Team members want and need to continuously **I**mprove their knowledge and skills. The team knows what information would benefit them, and they pay more attention to what they've chosen or requested.

G: [As the food is delivered] Anything else we need?
T: Another good week?

Gina's meeting feels casual and light but is organized and focused. She's prepared with a list of topics as well as reports and other useful information.

Getting team meetings started can be a challenge. Everyone is busy, it's difficult to find a day and time that works for everyone, and some team members won't understand and appreciate the value of the meetings.

Simply announcing that meetings will begin on a certain day works, but asking for opinions and input conveys respect, generates support, and can draw useful suggestions.

Starting Team Meetings
In an informal discussion with the team

M: I'd like to get everyone's input on an idea. I've been thinking a weekly meeting might improve our communication and help us work together.

B: What would we talk about?

M: Our results for the week, our successes and opportunities, team members' accomplishments, what each of us are working on, things we expect to come up in the next week, opportunities to help each other, ideas to make things work more smoothly, ...

L: It would be nice to know how we're doing overall and the challenges each of us are facing. We might be able to help each other.

Although Mike has already thought about instituting meetings, he asks the team to consider and debate the idea and is open to new thoughts.

D: I hate meetings. They keep us from doing our work.

M: Yes, I agree—they do interrupt our work. And that's why we'd want to keep them as concise and relevant as possible.

R: I think it would help me. I get a lot of phone questions I don't know the answers to and sometimes the information I give out is ... well, not the best.

D: I don't have time for meetings. I'm struggling to keep up already.

Agreement is rarely unanimous for anything. Mike is open to opposition because he knows he's not always right, and his team has learned they can express opposing opinions freely.

C: It might help us work more as a team. Sometimes it feels like we're working in silos with no communication or coordination.

M: **Any more thoughts?**

G: I can think of some things it would be useful to talk about.

M: **It sounds like the idea has some support even if it's not unanimous. Shall we try it?**

"Trying" new ideas is more conducive to team spirit and participation than imposing them. (It also offers a more graceful exit from ideas that don't work out.)

A trial put into motion usually remains until someone takes the initiative to stop it.

P: When?

M: **How about Tuesday mornings? We're all here on Tuesdays.**

D: Tuesdays are busy.

M: **Is there a better day?**

D: Not really. We're busy every day.

M: **OK, let's try Tuesdays at 8:30 then. I'll share some topic ideas with you by email. See what you think and what we should add or leave off.**

Mike asks for team input into the agenda both to draw their ideas and to encourage adoption of the meetings as a team project.

Chapter 10

Delegation

The most difficult transition for new managers is almost always from doing work, to seeing that work gets done.

Most of us are selected for management because we work hard. It's more than a habit, it's our personalities—it is who we are and impossible to change. When we see something that needs doing, we can't help ourselves—we do it.

But that also forms the dead-end many of us hit. Instead of organizing our teams to do the work, we work longer and harder, doing all the important tasks ourselves and as much of the rest as we can.

Meanwhile, our willing and eager teammates are left on the bench, idly watching. They get only busywork, quickly become bored and discouraged, and never develop to their potential.

Motivated team members leave for more meaningful work and a chance to progress; the less motivated stay, settling into a routine of little responsibility, and accepting boredom as the price of a paycheck.

Our previously admirable inclination to do work now threatens to derail our careers. We work long hours and holidays just to keep our heads above water while our unmotivated teams accomplish less than they should.

Why do we work so hard to keep our teams from helping us?

Because we think it's easier to do the work ourselves than to teach someone else. And, indeed, it does take time and effort to teach team members. But once they've got it, we've freed a recurring block of time to pursue other, often more important goals.

Because we fear it won't be done right. Team members do make mistakes, especially while learning a new job. But eventually they'll be able to do it as well as we do—better, if they do it more often.

Because we think they wouldn't do it the way we would. And it's true. Each person does things in their own way. But if they dependably get good results, their methods shouldn't concern us. We might even discover a better way.

Because it feels awkward asking someone else to do something we could do ourselves. We forget that our team members don't want to be on the sidelines. They want to Participate, contribute toward Objectives, and earn Respect. Being asked isn't an imposition—it's an honor, an expression of trust, an endorsement of abilities, and an opportunity to prove themselves.

Because we simply don't know how to ask. We can't find words we're comfortable with.

Asking isn't difficult.

> **M:** Our victory celebration is Tuesday and we need someone to…. Who would like to volunteer?

Notice that Mike didn't say, "I need someone to...." That would imply that the project and vision are his, and his people are simply his helpers. It's a **T**eam effort and team members share the **O**bjectives.

Many responsibilities require skills or experience, or are ongoing, and deserve more thought than just asking for volunteers. We should assign these to the people most appropriate to handle or learn them.

> **M:** Ed, we need someone to schedule maintenance on these machines to keep them operating smoothly. Would you be willing to handle that?

Most teams include several talented members who could handle almost any responsibility we give them. Delegating to them is tempting because they already know how to do the tasks and we know they'll do them correctly and reliably.

But our goal is not to have the most capable people on our team do every task. These people are valuable, and our supply is limited; we should carefully plan the best use of their time.

In most cases, the appropriate person is the least valuable team member who can do it accurately and reliably. A task more experienced team members would consider busywork is often prized by less experienced team members as an opportunity to **P**articipate, earn **R**espect, and **I**mprove. In addition to conserving our developed talent for more important tasks, we help everyone grow and increase in value, building a stronger and more capable team.

Asking someone to take a responsibility because we trust them to do it well makes it almost irresistible.

> **M:** Lisa, this report has to be accurate, and you're excellent with details. Could you take it over for us?

Complex responsibilities often take time and training to turn over.

> **M:** Cindy, you do a good job preparing the numbers for the monthly finance meeting, and you can answer questions about them better than I can. I'd like you to start going with me to that meeting. And, when you're comfortable with it, I'd like you to be our representative there.

Responsibilities that require stretching are opportunities to **I**mprove, earn **R**espect, and move up in the company.

Occasionally a team member will tell us they're too busy. If they truly are busy with more important tasks, we should respect that and look for a more appropriate person.

However, sometimes they simply need our help in delegating downward.

> **M:** I know you have a full schedule of responsibilities and I don't want to overload you. Would it help if we considered which of your current

responsibilities we might assign to someone else? You're a star on
our team and I'd like you to continue progressing in both skills and
experience.

What tasks should be delegated?

Some great managers delegate virtually everything.
They're not lazy—they simply want to free themselves to
solve problems, improve systems, coach team members, look
for opportunities, pursue innovations, work on special projects, etc. These managers and their teams are often the most
productive.

Other managers feel a few things should never be delegated; the list often includes personnel decisions, pay, budgets,
preparing and running team meetings, and reports to higher
ups. These are indeed important tasks and they need to be done
correctly.

But many managers successfully delegate these too, especially as they move higher in the company. There are no
fixed tasks for managers, and few that can't be delegated. A
manager is responsible for getting things done, not for doing
them.

The most effective method for choosing what we should
delegate is to list over a week or more every activity we're
involved in and the time spent on it. Then add the activities we
would do if we had time. Without consideration of who is going to take on the tasks we don't choose, select the tasks we
feel absolutely must be done by us. Prune the list aggressively,
leaving plenty of free time for unexpected challenges and innovations.

Only after our list is set, should we think about who will
take over the tasks we left.

This exercise almost always represents a major restructuring of our activities—and typically a turning point in our productivity and careers.

When we delegate a responsibility, we need to ensure our team member understands it and the expected outcome.

M: Thank you for taking this on. So we can confirm that I've explained it clearly, would you please send me an email with your understanding of it, the time frame, and the expected outcome? I want to help you get off on the right foot.

Although we should be clear about the expected outcome and schedule, we shouldn't tell them how they have to do it. That saps motivation and turns the task into busywork.

And we should follow up, particularly at first, to ensure their understanding was correct, they haven't run into problems or delays, and the result is as expected.

An ideal time for follow-up is during daily rounds.

M: How are you doing with your new responsibility, Paul?
   Any challenges or questions?
   Does it look like you're on schedule?
   If you'll show me the first couple, we'll be sure we're together.

Planning a project is the ideal time to put delegation skills to work.

Delegation for a Project
During the weekly team meeting:

M: Our customer open house is in a few weeks, so it's time to start planning. I made this list of responsibilities we'll need to cover.... What have I left out?

G: How about transportation?

T: I didn't hear renting tables.

M: Yes, you're both right. Let's add those.
OK, let's divide them. Frank, will you make note of these and email them to us?

F: (nods)

M: Karen, you've done a great job with decorations in the past. Do you want that?

K: Sure.

M: Tom, can you take getting the tables and setting up the hall?

T: OK.

M: Cindy, would you like to...?

C: Yes, but I'll need some help. Can Lisa work with me?

M: Lisa?

L: Sure.

M: Who would like to...?

....

M: Any other thoughts?
OK, sounds like we've got a good plan. We'll do a quick progress report at each weekly meeting. In the meantime, let me know if you have additional ideas or need something.

To ensure that repeating tasks can be delegated with minimal error and loss of experience in the future, we can have the people responsible for them create simple operating manuals. The manuals need not be elaborate or eloquent—just notes of the steps, lessons learned, and tips to avoid mistakes of the past. Good manuals make it possible to promote their writers to ever higher responsibilities.

For most of us, our accomplishments and our success as managers are limited only by our willingness to delegate.

Chapter 11

Coaching One-on-One

All employees want to know how they're doing—and every manager needs to ensure they do. Not just in general or overall, but in detail, for each aspect of the job, each skill, and each opportunity for improvement. Not sharing that information deprives the employees, the team, and the organization of their potential improvements.

One-on-one private meetings are a manager's opportunity to talk candidly with team members about their work, encourage their efforts, recognize their achievements, suggest improvements, and offer help.

One-on-ones work best on a regular schedule. Quarterly is a good minimum but more frequently is often appropriate. A manager might choose to meet with a new employee daily, a team member having trouble once or twice a week, and a reliable long-termer only quarterly.

An office is an ideal space for the meeting, but almost any private area can work—the team member's desk if private, a table in the corner, a conference room, a patio, etc. Sometimes ambient noise in a cafeteria or otherwise busy spot provides enough privacy.

One-on-One Meeting

M: Jackie, when you get a minute can you have a cup of coffee with me?

J: OK, I should be free in a few minutes.

Although Mike makes a point to meet with each of his team members at least once every 90 days, he doesn't schedule the meetings formally; he believes that creates anxiety and raises defenses. Instead he approaches his one-on-ones as casual conversations.

Other managers do schedule formal meetings and often ask their team members to bring reports, summarize the previous period, review progress on goals, and prepare a plan for the next period. That process is often suitable for managing managers.

A meeting with the manager is frightening for many employees; getting them to relax and speak freely is challenging. Most will carry on polite conversation but won't share any significant information until they're comfortable—and that can take some time and effort.

A casual atmosphere with coffee or a soft drink encourages open dialogue. Small talk, especially about something they're passionate about, helps them relax and speak freely.

In a little while Jackie appears at Mike's door.

M: Do you prefer coffee, latte, or Coke?

J: Latte sounds good.

M: We haven't talked in a while. How's life?

J: OK.

M: Is your daughter still involved in...?
J: Yes, she just.... We were really proud....
M: That's impressive. How did she...?
J: She....
M: Wow! It must be gratifying to see her do so well.
J: Yes, it is. [smiling now]

Children, hobbies, or favorite causes are good conversation starters. Sports teams, vacations, and leisure activities sometimes work. The weather and the news are weak topics, and politics are hazardous.

The old advice that managers should be distant with employees and avoid non-work topics is antiquated and offensive. It's OK to get to know our team members—and care about them! We spend a large part of our waking hours with them, often for years, and we depend on each other. We need understanding and trust. If they obviously enjoy talking about a subject, asking and being a willing listener are basic human courtesies.

Nevertheless, there are sometimes topics that team members aren't comfortable discussing with us. We should, of course, respect their privacy; those topics would be counterproductive in promoting conversation anyway. And, of course, any conversation bordering on sex or discrimination in any form is always off-limits.

Only after his team member is comfortable and begins speaking freely, does Mike move the conversation toward work.

He begins with a broad question to uncover ominous frustrations and dissatisfactions.

M: Are you happy with the way things are going at work?

Naturally he hopes for a positive response. When he gets it, he can move on to performance topics.

But he might get an answer like, "To be honest, ... [I was disappointed when..., my workload has gotten..., it's not much fun when..., I don't really enjoy..., the schedule has become more difficult now that..., I'm having trouble getting along with..., I was hoping I'd be promoted..., etc.]."

There's no point in discussing an employee's job performance and potential improvements if the employee is frustrated, unhappy with the job, or making other plans.

J: Well, actually there's something that's bothering me. I....
M: I see. I'm glad you're telling me about it. Tell me more.
J: ....
M: I understand. Anything else?
J: ....
M: Have you thought about how the problem could be resolved?
J: ....
M: OK, what if we.... Would that fix it?

Only after they've agreed on a plan or solution does Mike move on.

M: I know I miss some opportunities to thank you and recognize you for all you do but I want you to know that I appreciate you. You're a key player on the team and I have a lot of faith in you.
J: Thank you, Mike.

Starting the performance conversation with compliments boosts a team member's confidence and creates a positive atmosphere for open communication.

M: How do you feel you're doing overall?
J: I think pretty well. I feel like I can handle....

Asking a team member for his opinion of his work is less threatening than Mike offering his own assessment.

In most cases, the employee is pretty accurate, and Mike only has to agree.

M: Yes, I think so too. What aspects do you feel you're best at?
J: Probably....
M: I agree. And I've noticed you're also good at....

Acknowledging strengths builds credit to offset the discussion of potential improvements. If there are big improvements to be discussed, dwelling longer on strengths can be helpful.

If Mike conveys **R**espect for the employee's work, the employee should be comfortable discussing where he could improve.

M: What would you like to do better?
J: Well, I have trouble with....
M: I see. Which part is the challenge?
J: I just can't get....

Most employees recognize where their opportunities for improvement are, often better than we, as managers, do. If we've created a trusting atmosphere, they'll typically recite a pretty accurate list. And, since they want to Improve, they should welcome our support and encouragement.

M: I understand. What do you think you need to get better at it?

J: Probably just....

M: That makes sense. What can I do to help you?

J: I think I know what to do but I'll let you know if I need help.

Their ideas on how to make the improvements are usually the ones they're most likely to implement.

Sometimes, we can provide help—a book, a video, a course, the assistance of another team member, time with an experienced coworker, etc.

M: Anything else you'd like to learn or become better at?

If a team member doesn't mention an improvement Mike has in mind, he can bring it up.

M: How do you think you do with...?

J: Well, I could probably do better at that.

M: In what way?

J: I think I could....

An additional question or two usually evokes an opinion Mike can agree with.

However, occasionally, a team member thinks their performance is better than Mike does, and he simply has to disagree.

M: Paul, how do you think you're doing at getting the reports out on time?
P: Pretty well. I rarely miss the schedule.
M: How often would you say?
P: Not very often.
M: Hmm. Can you check that?
P: What do you mean?
M: Well, I noticed a couple of times in the last few weeks that the reports were a day or two late. One team member mentioned he doesn't like to use them because the information is sometimes old when he gets it.

Mike isn't adversarial or demoralizing. His focus is on a specific performance and never a judgment of the employee himself.

If they can't agree there's a problem, Mike can propose that the team member track the behavior for a while and report back.

P: Mike, I don't think that happens often.
M: OK, let's do this. Keep a list of the dates and times you send them out. In a couple of weeks, we can look at it together.
P: OK, but it'll probably just show that I'm right on time.
M: That would be perfect.

In most cases the tracking itself will correct the problem, and we don't need to discuss whose perception was correct.

Occasionally Mike needs to recommend a change a team member probably wouldn't think of.

M: **Ed, can I suggest something?**
E: Sure.
M: **I noticed you sometimes.... [get upset, procrastinate, forget to..., etc.]**
E: [nodding]
M: **Have you thought about...?**
E: Hmm.
M: **It really helps me when....**
E: Well, I'll try it.
M: **Let me know how it works for you.**

It's usually better to work on one major improvement or two to three minor improvements at a time, even when the list could contain many more. More than a few can be overwhelming and demoralizing to a team member.

A comfortable and open one-on-one is also the right time to discuss their long-term goals. (More on that in chapter 18, "Helping Them Outgrow Us.")

Then a little encouragement for their plan:

M: **I like the things you're working on and I'm eager to hear how it goes.**
J: I'll keep you posted.
M: **Is there anything I can do to help with them or your work?**
J: I'll let you know if I think of something.

Toward the end of the conversation, the team member should be most relaxed and sometimes willing to bring up questions or concerns they weren't comfortable discussing earlier.

M: Anything else you'd like to talk about while we're here?

And some final appreciation and respect.

M: Thanks again for all you do. You're a key contributor to our team and I really enjoy working with you.

The tone of Mike's one-on-one conversations is honest, respectful, encouraging, and helpful. He believes his people want to Improve their abilities and value, and his role is to assist them by providing encouragement, training, information, and support.

After each one-on-one meeting, we should make notes to help us continue the conversation in the future and remember what they are working on and how we can help.

Mike's One-on-One Outline

- Break the ice with casual conversation
- Check for overall satisfaction
- Compliment to create confidence
- Ask what the team member feels he does well
- Agree where appropriate and encourage
- Ask what employee feels he could improve
- Encourage a plan
- Make suggestions and offer help
- Thank and compliment

Chapter 12

Changing Behaviors

Tardiness. Absenteeism. Improper dress. Wasting time. Long smoking or coffee breaks. Disorganization. Procrastination. Failure to prioritize. Safety violations. Non-business internet use. Wasting supplies. Damaging equipment. Distracting coworkers. Excessive personal phone calls or texting. Offensive language. Off-color jokes. Extended lunches. Leaving stations unattended. There are more inappropriate work behaviors than could be listed here.

There is no such thing as a perfect employee (or manager). Our role as managers is to encourage our imperfect but talented and willing team of humans to achieve extraordinary results. We have to expect some behavioral challenges along the way.

Fortunately, not every infraction needs to be addressed. Those with insignificant consequences and that are unlikely to be repeated are often better overlooked. "Running a tight ship" is an admirable goal but not by being "an iron-fisted tyrant." Better to conserve our influence for more important issues.

Likewise, our long-term employees deserve some latitude. They rarely need us to explain what's expected, and they've proven their commitment to the team and its goals; we can sometimes assume unusual circumstances, at least for the first occurrence.

But most other inappropriate behaviors do need to be addressed, especially since what we choose to ignore often becomes standard practice.

But how do we do it? We sense the conversation will be awkward and embarrassing to the team member. We dread having it and we tend to put it off, hoping the problem will go away on its own.

Some managers procrastinate until they can no longer contain their frustration, finally blurting it out in ugly exasperation. A manager losing his temper is not an inspirational sight. The employee and everyone else who hears the outburst resents it as needlessly harsh. "If that was a concern, why didn't he just say so?"

A tempting workaround is a general announcement and reminder to the team. But that unnecessarily subjects the whole team to a negative and undeserved lecture. Most team members know who the message is for and recognize the method as an attempt to avoid a direct discussion—a poor example of the open communication we want to create.

Nor is it effective to joke or tease the employee about the behavior, to try to innocuously slip a recommendation for change into another conversation, or to send a message through other team members.

The only appropriate method for addressing a problem behavior is a private conversation, directly with the employee.

The tone should always be respectful and supportive, not confrontational. Our words and manner should reflect our belief that the employee is a willing team member, eager to do what he can to help the team achieve its goals.

A simple and inoffensive opening is mentioning that we noticed the behavior, asking about it, and allowing the employee to explain.

1st Conversation on Punctuality

*Haley, a new employee, shows up
for work 30 minutes late. Mike stops by her desk.*

M: Haley, I noticed you were late this morning. Is everything OK?
H: Yes, I'm sorry. It was.... [traffic, my alarm, car wouldn't start, etc.]
M: I see.

Asking sometimes reveals an unexpected reason for the behavior. A late employee might have had an accident, taken a child to the emergency room, or spent the night at the hospital with a sick parent. Expounding on the problem her lateness caused before finding this out would come across as insensitive and uncaring, especially to a team member already coping with a difficult situation.

The fine art of correcting behavior is applying just enough influence to change the behavior without creating resentment or an adversarial relationship. Better to err on the side of understatement than to come on too strong. We can elaborate further when necessary, but we can't take back the resentment of a perceived heavy hand.

Indicating we noticed the problem is often enough to correct the behavior, especially if the employee is aware of what's expected. If the employee doesn't know what's expected and why it's important, we can politely explain.

In most cases, nothing else is needed. A good team member will try not to disappoint us again.

If the problem recurs, we can again indicate we noticed and ask about it. If an acceptable reason isn't offered, we can mention the problem it causes, ask how they might avoid the problem behavior in the future, and offer our encouragement.

2nd Conversation on Punctuality

Haley is on-time for several days and then comes in 30 minutes late again. Mike finds an opportunity to talk with her privately.

M: **Haley, we missed you this morning. Did you have trouble again?**

H: Yes, unfortunately. I'm sorry. It was.... [traffic, ...,]

M: **When you're late, someone has to cover for you. Is there something you can do to ensure you make it on time?**

H: I guess I'll have to set my alarm a little earlier. I'll make sure it doesn't happen again.

M: **Thanks, Haley. I know you can do it.**

The third recurrence of a problem, especially in a short time, sometimes indicates a character flaw that we can't fix.

If it's a behavior we can't live with, it's time to politely remind them that we need a person in the job who performs appropriately and encourage them to be that person.

3rd Conversation on Punctuality

After coming in on-time for more than a week, Haley shows up 45 minutes late. Mike stops at her desk to talk while no one else is near.

M: **Haley, I was surprised to see you were late again this morning. Did something happen?**

H: I'm sorry, Mike. My.... [weak excuse]

M: **I'm worried because that's three times in a couple of weeks.**

H: Yes, I know.

M: **Our team really needs a person in that role who's dependable. Do you think you can do it?**

H: Yes, I can do it.

M: **Do you have a plan to fix it?**

H: Well, I'll....

M: OK, we're counting on you, Haley. If there's something I can do to help, let me know.

H: Thanks, Mike. I won't let you down.

There's never a need to explicitly threaten an employee with termination. The understanding is always clear that if they can't or won't do the job, we have to get someone who can. Several discussions are sufficient notice that their past performance is not adequate.

Companies and organizations at high risk of employment lawsuits sometimes want it spelled out in writing for the employee, as discussed below, but few employees really fail to understand the situation.

Contrary to the popular misconception, reprimanding or imposing discipline won't turn an employee into the team member we need. Discipline and threats imply that the employee follows the rules only to avoid punishment. If an employee accepts that implication, they'll do the minimum necessary to get by in all their work.

Such an adversarial relationship is the opposite of the team commitment we need and work hard to create. What's worse, the adversarial attitude sometimes spreads through a team like a cancer.

If a few conversations don't correct an inappropriate behavior, the employee simply isn't the team member we need, and we should make a change.

Since conversations to change behaviors are among the most uncomfortable of a manager's responsibilities, let's watch Mike handle another.

His formula for the first occurrence is to mention he noticed, ask what happened, and, if necessary, explain the problem it causes.

1ˢᵗ Conversation on Dependability

Paul is responsible for preparing the selection room for appointments.

M: **Paul, I noticed the room wasn't ready this morning when our customer arrived. Did something happen?**

P: Well, I got interrupted just as I started working on it.

M: **I see. We seem disrespectful when we make our customers wait for us to get organized.**

P: I'm sorry. I'll have it ready next time.

M: **Thanks, Paul.**

If the problem occurs again, Mike says he noticed, asks what happened, explains a problem it causes, asks for a plan, and offers encouragement.

2ⁿᵈ Conversation on Dependability

A week later Mike sees customers again standing outside the selection room. Later in the day he stops at Paul's desk.

M: **Paul, I noticed people were waiting for you to get the selection room ready again this morning. What happened?**

P: Unfortunately I got a call from a supplier and it took longer than I expected.

M: **It was a little embarrassing for the team and uncomfortable for our customers.**

P: I'm sorry.

M: **What can you do to make sure the room is ready from now on?**

P: I guess I need to start earlier to allow for interruptions.

M: **Can you do that?**

P: I'll make sure to.

M: **Thanks, Paul. We're counting on you.**

Although Mike's disappointment is surely growing, he remains respectful and encouraging. If he feels like letting his frustrations out, he knows it would serve no useful purpose and would only damage the pride he wants Paul to take in his work.

If the problem continues, Mike indicates he noticed, asks what happened, expresses concern, states the need for a dependable person to do the job, asks for a plan, and offers encouragement.

3rd Conversation on Dependability

Mike sees Paul in a rush again to prepare the room for a customer who has already arrived. After the appointment, Mike invites Paul to his office.

M: **Paul, I was surprised to see that the selection room wasn't ready again this morning. What happened?**

P: I'm sorry. I was helping Gina with a delivery problem and I lost track of time.

M: **I'm concerned because that's the third time. When we're not ready for our customers, we make them feel unwelcome and waste their time. We really need a person in that job who can have it ready consistently. Do you think you're going to be able to do it?**

P: Yes, I can do it.

M: **What will you do differently?**

P: I'm going to start earlier and not allow myself to be interrupted.

M: **Have you thought about setting it up the day before?**

P: That's a good idea. I'll do that.

M: We're really counting on you, Paul. If there's something I can do to help, please let me know.

If Paul doesn't respond after these conversations, he probably isn't capable, and Mike will have to make a change.

Occasionally a team member doesn't understand the importance of what's expected and needs a more extensive explanation. Everyone is more committed when they understand the whys.

1st Conversation on Off-color Jokes

Tom is perennially the team's top salesman and is well respected inside and outside the company. He's gregarious, popular, and fun—and often tells improper jokes. After hearing him tell one, Mike discretely invites Tom to his office to talk.

M: Tom, your sales are excellent, and I always appreciate your positive attitude. But there is something I need to talk to you about.

T: OK, what's up?

M: I'm concerned that some of your jokes might make some of our coworkers uncomfortable.

T: Everyone laughs at my jokes. What's the problem?

M: Sex, race, religion, national origin, etc. are sensitive subjects and we have to be careful not to offend anyone.

T: Has someone complained about something I said?

M: No, fortunately not. And it's something you and we really need to avoid. Company policy on that is rigid, and the laws are tough. A complaint requires a formal warning and sometimes a job reassignment. The consequences of a second complaint are especially severe.

T: I see. Well, I hope I haven't offended anyone. I'll choose my jokes more carefully in the future.

M: I appreciate that, Tom. That's exactly the attitude I've learned to expect from you.

If an otherwise good team member repeats the behavior, we might assume he didn't understand the rules and reasons.

2nd Conversation on Off-color Jokes
A week later Mike hears Tom tell a gathering of teammates another joke that might offend. Later Mike catches Tom in private.

M: Tom, you didn't forget our conversation last week, did you?

T: Not at all. I haven't offended anyone, have I?

M: That joke you told a little while ago might offend someone.

T: They all laughed so I don't think it did.

M: Yes, I noticed they laughed too. But unfortunately that doesn't mean they weren't embarrassed or uncomfortable.

T: I don't mean to offend anyone. If I do, I'll certainly apologize.

M: I wish it were that simple, Tom. Remember we talked about how tough company procedures and the law are. I've printed them out for you to take with you and read. Some of the consequences are pretty serious.

T: You mean I can't tell jokes?

M: I don't mean that at all. We enjoy your jokes. It makes the workplace more fun. We just can't tell jokes about sex, race, religion, etc.

T: OK, I'll be more careful. It's OK to tell them to Dan and Paul, isn't it, especially since they tell similar ones to me?

M: I know it's unlikely they'd be offended but it's just not worth the risk, Tom. You have such a large repertoire of jokes. Can you just choose some that aren't about sex?

T: Those aren't the good ones. [smile] But I understand what you're saying. I'll clean up my act and encourage the others to do the same.

M: **Thanks, Tom. I knew I could count on you. And thanks for setting the
example for the others. They look up to you.**

If the situation occurs a third time, the employee either
isn't comprehending the situation and its seriousness, or can't
control his behavior. In either case, we have an obligation to
explain it as clearly as possible.

3rd Conversation on Off-color Jokes
*After hearing Tom tell another improper joke in the hall,
Mike invites Tom to his office.*

M: **Tom, you're our best sales person and everyone loves working with
you. But your jokes really have me worried.**

T: Did someone complain?

M: **No, fortunately not. If they did, we'd have serious problems. Do you
recall what the law and company procedures say?**

T: Well, I probably didn't read them as carefully as I should have.

M: **Let's go over them together. I think it's worth our time. Here's what
the law says…. And company procedure says….**

T: Wow! That sounds like overreaction to me.

M: **It *is* tough, and, as you see, it doesn't allow us much wiggle room.
Losing you would be a huge setback for our whole team, Tom, and
create some major problems for both you and me.**

T: I guess I didn't realize it was that serious.

M: **I think it is and it really has me worried. What can you do to keep us
out of trouble?**

T: I guess I have to just stop telling those kinds of jokes.

M: That would resolve it and we could all rest easier. But I know you love those jokes. Do you really think you can do it?

T: From the sound of it, I don't have a choice.

M: I think you're right and I appreciate your willingness. I hope you'll continue to tell jokes–but clean ones, please.

T: Thanks for letting me know about this. I didn't realize how serious it was.

M: I'm glad you've got it now, Tom. You can do this.

After every behavior-change conversation, we should make notes. For companies at low risk of lawsuits, a simple dated note is often enough for our own reference as well as the rare legal challenge.

However, for many companies and organizations, harassment and employment lawsuits are a constant concern. As a result, most of these companies require procedures and documentation to protect themselves.

Such requirements add a layer of challenge to the positive team environment we want to create. The formality and documentation can make a workplace feel like a legal battleground between employees and management—the opposite of the cooperation and shared commitment we want to create. In addition, the required procedures visibly tie a manager's hands, often allowing poor team members to stay on longer than they should, and encouraging them to challenge the manager's authority.

Nevertheless, behavioral conversations and terminations sometimes lead to legal actions, and defending the company against them is expensive and time consuming. We not only have to be careful not to break a law, we have to be prepared to *prove* we didn't break it.

Documentation is particularly important when an employee repeats an inappropriate behavior multiple times or appears to be approaching termination.

Documenting Behavior Conversations

Mike talked with Ed after a couple of anger outbursts, but the problem has come up again. During Mike's conversation with Ed:

M: Company procedures require me to fill out a form for both of us to sign, Ed. I've tried to do it as fairly as possible.

E: You're writing me up for this?!

M: It's a standard procedure that we're obligated to follow, Ed. In the long term, it shouldn't make any difference if you've got this under control.

E: I just don't like having that in my file.

M: I know. I don't like having to do it either. But we'll get through it and it shouldn't interfere with your work.

Employment law is too complicated and specialized to attempt any specific legal advice here; in most cases, we're safe when we follow our company's prescribed procedures.

If our companies don't have guidelines, we need to familiarize ourselves with the laws, so we can recognize and avoid potentially troublesome situations.

Chapter 13

Tackling Underperformance

Employees who don't get as much done as they should are one of management's perennial challenges—and one that's tempting to overlook. The team member is often amiable, dependable, and cooperative, and rarely bends or breaks the rules. They just don't get the results we need.

"Nice" management in no way means ignoring underperformance. If we do, we mislead the team member into thinking they're doing OK and deprive them of the opportunity to make needed improvements. Worse, we frustrate other team members by holding back the team's results and lowering its standards. And we are remiss in our responsibilities to our organizations to get results.

Poor performance must be addressed, and the only appropriate way is directly with the employee, in a private one-on-one meeting.

Most poor performers recognize their shortcomings but asking is a good way to open the conversation and test their awareness of expectations.

Underperformance #1

After six months on the job, Dan has fallen behind entering orders.
Mike invites him to his office to talk.

M: **Dan, how're you doing with the orders?**

D: OK, I think.

M: **How current are you?**

D: Probably within a few days.

M: **What are the standards we're trying to stay within?**

D: I remember you and Sam told me it needs to be current daily. Unfortunately, I've gotten a little behind on that lately.

Dan confirms he's aware of the expectations and knows he's not meeting them.

Now they need to identify the cause.

M: **What do you feel is holding you back?**

D: Well, I've just been busy with other things.

M: **I see. Do you feel you have too many responsibilities?**

D: Not really; I can handle them.

M: **Which do you feel is most important?**

D: Well, this one is.

M: **What do you think the problem has been?**

D: I guess I just haven't focused on it.

Dan's analysis seems correct, so Mike asks for a plan to address the problem.

M: **OK, I understand. What do you need to do to fix it?**

D: I guess I just need to make the orders my priority, do them first, and not get distracted by other things until they're done.
M: **Makes sense. Do you think you can do that?**
D: Yes, I'll do it.
M: **Is there anything you need?**
D: I don't think so.

The solution most likely to be executed is usually the one the team member comes up with. Mike feels Dan's solution is reasonable, so he goes along with it.

M: **OK. I'll check with you each day until you get caught up.**
D: I can probably be caught up by Thursday.
M: **That would be great. This is important to our team, Dan. We're counting on you. Thanks for taking it seriously.**

Follow-up serves as a reminder to the team member and allows us to confirm the problem has been fixed.

In some cases, calling the team member's attention to the problem, asking for a plan to take care of it, and following up is enough to resolve underperformance issues.

However, performance problems that appear once often recur. When they do, we need to spot and address them quickly, before they become habit.

Underperformance #2
Dan has fallen behind again. Mike invites him to his office.

M: **How are you doing with the orders, Dan?**
D: I was doing fine, but I've gotten a little behind again.

Mike asks, both to understand Dan's perspective, and in case there's a problem Mike isn't aware of.

M: I see. What happened?
D: Well, I just got busy with other things.
M: What things are interrupting you?
D: Just my other responsibilities—but I understand the orders are supposed to be my priority.

The cause hasn't changed, and Mike confirms Dan is aware of it.

Since this is the second occurrence, Mike adds emphasis by explaining the problems it causes.

M: When the orders aren't entered daily, we can't tell what we've sold, what we need, and how we're doing. That can cause us to make some expensive mistakes.
D: I understand.

Then they need a plan.

M: What do you think you need to do to keep them up?
D I just need to focus on it and not allow myself to be interrupted.
M: OK. Is there anything you need from me?
D: No, I think I have everything.

Mike schedules follow-up.

M: OK. Please let me know how you're doing each day until you're caught up. After that, I'd like you to email me every Tuesday and Friday morning with the status.

D: OK, I'll do that.

Having the team member initiate feedback encourages them to make progress before reporting. (Mike makes a note on his to-do list in case Dan forgets to follow through.)

And finally, some encouragement.

M: You can do this, Dan. I picked you for this team and I want you to succeed. We're all counting on you.

Typically, Dan won't want to disappoint Mike or the team, and will try to meet expectations.

Some people, however, won't be able to live up to the expectations. The problem isn't bad intentions; most mean to please. Often the task just isn't in their nature—it's not their personality.

Personalities are part of a person's core definition and have a powerful influence on the work they do. People can temporarily make themselves do work they're not suited for, but their personalities pull them back like tempered steel to their natural inclinations.

To illustrate, an accountant who is a "born salesman" is almost too odd to imagine; meanwhile, the paperwork of any good salesman is enough to drive an accountant to drink. They're different personalities. With some effort, both can learn the basic skills of the other. But the salesman will quickly tire of numbers and be drawn to people, while the accountant will quickly tire of people and take refuge in the numbers. In the wrong job, both will struggle and be unhappy. In the right one, they'll be productive, valuable, successful, and happy.

Not being suited for one job doesn't mean a team member isn't suited for any work. There's appropriate work for every personality. Job satisfaction, work quality, and general happiness depend on finding it.

In the spirit of open communication and fairness, we should discuss a possible work mismatch with an underperforming team member. Often it will prompt them to consider more appropriate and satisfying work. Occasionally we can help them find a better match within our team or the company.

If their mind is set on their current job, the discussion will at least allow them to think about the changes they need to make to do the job appropriately. It also ensures that, if we have to take them off the team, it won't seem an unfair surprise.

Underperformance #3

Dan has fallen behind for the third time in six months.
Mike asks him to join him in his office.

M: Dan, do I understand correctly that you're behind with orders again?

D: Just a little. I can catch up quickly.

M: How far behind are you?

D: Maybe a couple of days.

M: Can you check on that and give me an exact time?

D: Well, I'm caught up through last Monday.

M: So, you're four days behind?

D: Yes, I think so.

Dan knows the expectations and seems reluctant to admit he's not meeting them.

M: **Is there something that's keeping you from staying current?**
D: Not really. I just got busy with other things. I'm sorry.

By now Mike suspects Dan's failure to prioritize correctly is due to Dan preferring other activities to this one.

M: **Dan, you're a smart guy but it seems to me your heart isn't in this. Have you thought about whether this is the right kind of work for you?**

Raising the idea that a team member might not be suited for a job seems awkward, but Mike's question is honest and meant to be helpful. Preceding it with a compliment makes it less difficult.

D: What do you mean? I can do it.
M: **I know you're capable, Dan. But perhaps these tasks aren't things you like doing. If so, that doesn't reflect poorly on you. Each of us is suited to different kinds of work. When we find what's right for us, we're happier and do it better.**
D: I've got to work, Mike. And I've always been able to do whatever I put my mind to.

The idea of a job-personality mismatch comes as a surprise to many people—they've never thought about it.

M: I understand, and you can do this, too, when you focus on it. But that doesn't mean you enjoy doing it. Having trouble getting started and staying on task is often a sign that the work isn't a good match.

D: What else would I do?

M: That usually takes some thought. Career counselors specialize in helping people find the right work. If you like, I can.... [help you find a counselor, arrange an appointment for you, have the company provide that for you]. Once we've found what kind of work suits you, maybe I can help you find it.

Sometimes there's suitable work for an underperforming employee within our team or the company. In the right role, they sometimes become skilled and valuable long-term employees.

However, we should ensure that the new job is really a fit and something they will do well, and not just an easy method to move them out of the way or off our teams. Putting them where underperformance is less noticeable is not a fix for us or for them, and transferring the problem to someone else is bad karma that's rarely left unpaid.

It can take some time for a team member to absorb the idea that they're better suited for some kinds of work than others.

D: I really like this job.

M: What do you like about it, Dan?

D: Well, ...it pays well, the benefits are good, and I like the hours.

M: But what about the work? Do you enjoy doing it and take pride in what you accomplish? Or do you just put up with it for the pay, benefits, and hours?

D: I have a family, Mike. I have to work.

M: I understand but that shouldn't be a sentence. When we find the right work, we like doing it, do it better, are respected for it, and can earn more.

People who haven't experienced a right job often believe that work is doing things they dislike in exchange for the means to do things they like. "That's why it's called work," they say. Tragically, many never discover that they can enjoy work too, if they find work they're suited for.

D: I just can't afford to change jobs right now, Mike.
M: OK, I understand. These are some challenging thoughts and it can take a while to get used to them. But I would like you to think about it.

We should expect resistance at first, sometimes even complete rejection. At best, our conversation only starts the thought process.

But it's a process an underperforming team member needs to begin. The sooner he finds the right work, the happier and more productive he'll be.

M: In the meantime, let's do this. You know that keeping orders current is important to the team and that we need a person in that job we can depend on. If you feel you can do it, we can try again.
D: I can do it.
M: OK, we'll try again. And, if you decide you want to do something else, I'll.... [support you in the change, help you discover what work suits you, help you find a job you enjoy].
D: Thanks, Mike. I'll get it right.

M: We're pulling for you. If you want to talk, I'm here.

Typically, the team member will resolve to do better—and will improve, at least temporarily. At the same time, they'll usually begin thinking about other options and sometimes find something more suitable.

We've been honest and hopefully helpful with them. If they leave, their departure should be amiable and respectful. And if we were correct and they find work that's a better match, the rest of their work life should be happier, more productive, and more rewarding.

Instances in which the employee neither improves nor leaves for more appropriate work are rare. When they do occur, we have to make the change for them. Leaving them in an underperforming role is not fair to our team or our organization. We should do it respectfully (chapter 17)—but we must do it.

As with every important conversation, we should make notes afterward that include the date, what was discussed, the employee's response, and what was agreed upon. The notes remind us in our follow-up conversations and allow us to encourage our team members in the future. But they're also necessary, unfortunately, in termination and discrimination actions.

Occasionally a long-term, capable team member goes into a slump.

These team members usually don't need much guidance from us. In most cases we only need to mention that we noticed and offer help.

Uncharacteristic Underperformance
Mike talks privately with Sam at his desk.

M: Sam, you don't seem yourself lately. Is everything OK?

S: What do you mean?

M: Well, the proposal you wrote Monday didn't seem up to your usual standards. And yesterday you missed the deadline on…. I thought something might be wrong.

S: Actually, I've been having some problems at home. I think everything's going to be OK, but you're right—I haven't been as focused the last couple of weeks.

M: Is there anything I can do to help?

S: I appreciate it, Mike, but I'm getting through it. And I'll try not to let it affect my work.

M: I understand. You're a mainstay of our team, Sam, and we're here for you if you need us. Please let us know if there's something we can do for you.

Almost everyone goes through challenging times at some point in life. Those who have been loyal to us and the organization are especially deserving of our patience, consideration, and help.

Chapter 14

Dealing with Mistakes

We have to expect mistakes; nobody is perfect.

Insisting on perfection is usually counterproductive. When employees are afraid to make mistakes, they work slowly and don't attempt new methods or skills. Allowing enough latitude to make occasional mistakes promotes learning, innovation, ingenuity, and confidence.

Nevertheless, as managers, our reaction to a mistake is often frustration, followed by wondering (hopefully not aloud), "What the hell was she thinking?" or "How could he be so dumb?"

Our employees are seldom as dumb as a mistake makes them seem. However obvious a mistake may be after the fact, the choices that led to it typically were not. Often, we would have made the same choice in similar circumstances.

If we summarily blame an employee for a mistake without allowing them to explain, we risk our relationship with them—they rarely forget our misjudgment of them. Neither an apology nor time makes up for it.

Some mistakes don't need to be addressed. The employee knows what went wrong and how to avoid it in the future. Elaborating on the obvious would only create embarrassment and resentment. Our team members recognize and appreciate benign inattention when appropriate.

If we have to acknowledge an error, we can express confidence in the employee's ability to fix it.

M: We all make mistakes. I'm sure you can take care of it.

But many other mistakes do require our guidance. Sometimes the mistake isn't apparent, the solution isn't obvious, there are consequences and repercussions the team member isn't aware of, etc.

We should keep in mind that mistakes are unintentional—the team member was trying to do his job correctly and simply made an error. Our purpose isn't to assign blame or to scold, but to help the employee recognize the mistake, what caused it, and how to prevent it in the future.

Mike's format for dealing with mistakes is to indicate he noticed, ask how it happened, check whether the damage has been corrected, ask for a plan to avoid future occurrences, and offer encouragement.

First Mistake
During his daily rounds, Mike talks to Will
about a package Will shipped to the wrong customer.

M: Will, I heard we had a mix-up in shipping.

W: Yes, unfortunately I....

M: OK, we all make mistakes. How did it happen?

W: I guess I just....

M: I see. How will you fix it?

W: I've already.... And I'll....

M: **Sounds good. And how can you prevent that mistake in the future?**

W: I'm going to double-check....

M: **Sounds like you've got this, Will. Let me know if I can help.**

Allowing the team member to fix his mistake and asking for his plan for preventing it in the future keeps the responsibility with him and conveys respect and trust.

If the problem recurs in a short time, Mike confirms that the team member understands how the mistake is occurring, ensures the damage is corrected, and that his plan to avoid it is viable.

Repetition of a Mistake
A week later Mike hears another package was shipped to the wrong destination.

M: **Will, did we have another mis-shipment?**

W: Yes, I'm sorry, Mike.

M: **How did it happen?**

W: Well, I just got in a hurry and didn't check....

M: **Have you straightened it out with the customer?**

W: Yes, I....

M: **Do you think your plan is enough to head off the problem in the future?**

W: It should be. I just have to follow it.

M: **OK. Anyone can make a mistake; we just have to learn from them, so we don't repeat them.**

W: Thanks, Mike. I'll get it right.

M: **You can do it, Will. I believe in you.**

If the team member continues to make similar mistakes, we have to consider whether he's right for the job.

By now, the team member should realize his performance isn't adequate, and an open and honest dialogue about it sometimes comes as a relief.

Multiple Repetitions of a Mistake
After several shipments to wrong customers, Mike has a private conversation with Will.

M: Will, I know you're trying and I can tell you're frustrated. Have you considered that this job might not be a match for what you're best at?

W: What do you mean?

M: Every person is by nature good at some things, but no one is good at everything. The key to success is finding and doing what you do well.

W: Are you saying I can't do this job?

M: I don't know that for sure but if it were true, it wouldn't reflect poorly on you. It's just part of the process of finding what's right for you.

W: But I like this job and I need the money.

M: I understand. But what about the work itself? Do you enjoy it? Or does it frustrate you? In the long run, we're better off finding what really suits us; it allows us to enjoy our work, do it better, move up in our careers, and be respected for our abilities.

W: What else could I do?

M: You're smart. I'm confident there are a lot of things you can do. Career counselors specialize in helping people find the right work and many people say personality tests have helped them discover their special abilities. I can help you arrange either of those if you like.

W: That's a lot to think about.

M: I understand. Please do think about it. We can talk more whenever you like.

Personalities and work mismatches are discussed more extensively in Chapter 13, "Tackling Underperformance." It's a very real phenomenon we should watch for—for the benefit of our people, our teams, and our organizations.

It can take a team member some time to accept that a job is a mismatch. When he does, he'll almost always begin exploring more appropriate work.

Our responsibility as managers is to be open and honest in assessing their performance and encouraging concerning their options.

Chapter 15

Employee Disputes

Even an excellent team, committed to the same results, has an occasional disagreement. Seldom is it due to anyone's malevolent intentions, or to one person being right and one wrong. Most often disagreements are simply differences in information.

Some people feel our job as manager is to step into arguments, gather the facts, issue a judgment, and declare the dispute settled. But does that really resolve a disagreement? Almost any solution we choose will be resented by at least one of the parties. Hard feelings not only remain but are aggravated by our involvement. The battle lingers, and each side surreptitiously looks for chances to even the score or sabotage the other.

Others believe in creating a therapy session, getting all the complaints and hard feelings out on the table, trusting that will lead to an amiable understanding. It's a slow and painful process, and summoning up old grievances risks renewing forgotten hostilities.

Mike follows a different method.

Dispute Resolution
Tom catches Mike during his daily rounds.

T: Mike, I've got a problem I need your help with.

M: **Sure. What you got?**

T: Karen thinks the Jackson deal should be hers because she spent a lot of time on it. But the rules are clear.

M: **I see. And she's upset?**

T: Hasn't talked to me in two days.

M: **Not good. You two depend on each other.**

T: Right. Can you explain to her that the rules are the rules?

Tom subscribes to the theory that the boss need only issue an opinion and the dispute is over.

M: **I could, but it's not going to solve the bigger problem which is the relationship between you.**

T: Well, something needs to happen because right now we're working against each other. What do you recommend?

M: **I suspect it's going to take one of you making a peace gesture and offering a compromise.**

Mike knows a dispute is over only when the two parties decide they want to get along. All he can do is encourage them to work it out.

T: That seems unlikely considering some of the things that were said.

M: **Yeah, it's going to take a big person to do it.**

T: Really big!

M: Do you want me to talk to Karen and suggest the two of you get together to work it out?

T: No, it's probably better if I take the lead. I just need to figure out how I'll approach it.

M: I appreciate your willingness, Tom. You and Karen make a good team working together.

Team members can usually find a better compromise than any we might suggest. When they do, they're more likely to get along and avoid disagreements in the future.

Some employees attract an abnormal number of disagreements.

Sometimes, the problem is a lack of information and understanding. Those doing specialty work often don't comprehend the challenges and complexities outside their areas. Cross training or putting them into temporary task groups sometimes improves their understanding and relationships.

Occasionally, it's an aggressive style or an outspoken manner. Opportunities to get to know each other often resolve these. When we learn each other's styles, we accept and adapt to them.

But combativeness can also spring from deep psychological issues that nurture cynicism, suspicion, and distrust. Long-term solutions to these are more difficult—sometimes beyond our means.

A chronically contentious employee keeps hostilities stirred up and damages the spirit of a team.

A Contentious Team Member
Mike pays Ed a visit.

M: Ed, I understand you and Ann are having a dispute.

E: Yes, we are. I'm really tired of her sloppy paperwork. I have to be a detective just to figure out what she means.

M: I see. Did you discuss it with her?

E: I told her I couldn't read her work and that's the truth. I also said if she continued turning it in that way I wasn't going to process it anymore.

M: I guess she didn't respond well to that?

E: She said I have no right to talk to her like that, and if she had to process her own work she would, just so she doesn't have to deal with me.

Team members sometimes learn from their mistakes, so Mike asks.

M: Would you handle it the same way if you had it to do over again?

E: I don't see why not.

If Ed had resolved to change his approach, Mike would shift the conversation to encouragement.

But Ed hasn't.

M: Ed, your work is accurate and reliable. But I'm concerned about how you get along with your teammates.

E: What do you mean?

M: I believe that's three arguments with coworkers in the last month.

E: It might be, but everything I said to them was true.

Some people feel as long as what they say is true they're not responsible for the consequences. (Their marriages are usually short.)

M: It's not a matter of right and wrong, Ed. We simply can't get good results when team members are mad at each other or refuse to deal with each other.

E: You're acting like this is all my fault.

M: Ed, team members are going to have disagreements, but they need to discuss them respectfully and work them out. Do you feel you've discussed them respectfully? Or have you gotten angry and offended your coworkers?

E: If you knew what they did you'd be angry too.

M: Perhaps I would, but I'd do my best never to show it. Anger doesn't solve problems; it escalates them and damages relationships.

E: Well, what am I supposed to do with these people who aren't doing their jobs correctly?

Although Mike prefers that his teammates come up with the solutions they implement, it seems unlikely in this case.

M: Try this: Before you speak, take a little time, cool off, and think about how they're likely to respond to the words you choose. The goal is to make your point in a way that makes them want to work with you to fix the problem.

E: I don't see how I can tell them these things any other way.

M: It's not that hard to be nice, Ed. You just have to slow down and think before you speak.

Ed is a tough case. His uncompromising style and habit of offending coworkers likely come from deep within his psyche. If so, Mike will have trouble changing him.

Nevertheless, Mike shares the information and encourages him to try.

M: Ed, your work is good. But doing your own work is only part of the job. We work as a team. Your job requires cooperating with and helping your teammates.

E: Not easy.

M: It takes some effort and flexibility, Ed, but you can do it.

E: If you say so.

M: Please give it your best. I'll check with you over the next few days to see how it's going.

Communication, coordination, and understanding are essential for team results. While nothing we can say or do can force team members to like each other, we can express our preference clearly and encourage them to resolve their differences. If that's not enough, we have to remove the chronic agitators.

Most team members want to get along and will do what they can to maintain a drama-free, cooperative workplace.

Chapter 16

Performance Appraisals

Many organizations require annual or semi-annual performance reviews—and most managers despise them. Some of us say the reviews are unnecessary, claiming our regular communication is sufficient. On rare occasions it is.

Far more of us dislike them because we haven't been communicating and we fear the reviews will be awkward or even confrontational.

Despite our misgivings, performance reviews are excellent opportunities to communicate openly and honestly with each team member about their performance. If we've already been communicating, the reviews are an easy confirmation of what we've been saying. If we haven't been communicating, the reviews are an opportunity to fix it—to open the channels of communication, create understanding, offer guidance, provide encouragement, express appreciation, and help our team members reach their potential.

Performance reviews are also useful as a basis for salary increases and promotions. And occasionally they serve as a warning for underperformers or set the stage for the termination of an uncooperative or inappropriate team member.

Mike sets up his performance appraisals with a note or email.

Scheduling Performance Appraisals

From: Mike
To: Our ABC Team
Re: Performance Appraisals

Team,

It's time again for our performance appraisals. Please check your calendar and let me know when during the next two weeks you're available. The meeting should take about 30 minutes, but we can spend more time if there's something you'd like to discuss.

I've attached a blank copy of the appraisal form. If you'll fill in your thoughts beforehand, it will make it easier for us to complete the final version together.

Please review your previous performance appraisal and we'll discuss how you've progressed.

Also, give some thought to your self-improvement plan and how you'd like to grow in your job. If there are projects you're interested in, responsibilities you'd like to take on, or skills you'd like to learn, this is a good chance to discuss them.

I'm proud of our team and look forward to positive conversations.

Mike

Performance appraisals are more productive when both we and our team members prepare.

As managers, we need to review previous forms and notes, refresh our memories of the team member's successes and shortcomings, consider what abilities and behaviors the team member could improve, think about how we can encourage and help them, and plan our presentation.

Team members need to think about how they're performing, where their opportunities are, what goals are appropriate, how they want to pursue them, and what help they might need.

Having team members fill in the review form beforehand encourages them to think carefully and realistically about their performance and what they might improve.

The conversation of a performance appraisal is similar to the one-on-one meetings discussed in Chapter 10, "Coaching One-on-One," so it's abbreviated here.

A Performance Appraisal
Lisa comes to Mike's office for their scheduled performance review.
After they exchange pleasantries:

M: I know you've been thinking about, maybe even worrying about, this performance appraisal. Before we get into it, I want to tell you that I really appreciate your [great attitude, willingness to do whatever it takes, ability to..., reliability, etc.] For example, when....

Mike knows performance appraisals are intimidating. He tries to make his team members comfortable, so they can speak openly.

M: Let's start with the notes you made. Which things do you feel you do well?

L: Well, I think I'm pretty good at....
M: **Yes, you are. And that's valuable to the team. What else?**
L: ....
M: **You didn't mention.... I think you're good at that, too.**

Starting with positives and successes creates confidence and gets the conversation off on a good foot.

Establishing positives makes it less intimidating for team members to discuss their shortcomings.

M: **And which things do you feel are opportunities for improvement?**
L: I think I could do better at....

Usually their assessment is close to Mike's and he only has to agree.

But occasionally he needs to dig deeper.

M: **Let's talk about that for a minute. What do you think a good goal for that would be?**
L: Probably.... [a turnaround time of..., an error rate below..., holding expenses to..., etc.]

If they cite a reasonable goal, Mike can agree.

If they're new to the job or haven't seen others do it, they might not realize what's appropriate or possible. Sometimes Mike offers some guidance.

M: In the past we've been able to.... Do you think you could reach that?
L: Hmm. I don't know. I'll have to think about how to do it.
M: Would it help to...?
L: I can try that.

On rare occasions, Mike simply has to disagree with their assessment.

M: Interesting that you feel that way. I've noticed that.... For example, ...

Instead of offering a generalized opinion of the team member personally that might be demoralizing, he cites specific situations and performances.

Mike tries to make his performance appraisals more than just reviewing past performance and documenting results—he likes to include plans for improvement.

M: What do you think you can do to get better at that?
L: Well, I think I can....
M: That sounds good. Is there something I can do to help? Anything you need?

And he reviews the resolutions of previous performance appraisals and one-on-one meetings to keep planned improvements on track.

M: During our last meeting you said you wanted to work on…. How has that gone?

Perhaps the biggest threat to the usefulness of performance appraisals is appraisal inflation—rating everyone "meets expectations" or above to avoid disappointment or confrontation.

If we don't discuss performance and potential improvements openly and honestly during performance reviews, we probably aren't doing it at all. If so, we're remiss in our most important responsibility as managers—to help our people, our teams, and our companies improve, perform their best, and reach their potential.

M: In fairness I think we should rate this "Needs improvement." But I believe you have the potential to do it well. What can I do to help you with it?

It's especially important to be honest and accurate about performance and shortcomings in performance reviews because they often become prime legal documents in termination, harassment, and discrimination actions.

When we communicate regularly with our team members, the outcome of performance reviews isn't a surprise. They are simply another opportunity to show appreciation and respect, and to discuss how the team member can improve and advance.

Chapter 17

Firing

Most managers say firing is the most uncomfortable task they face.

The message is simple and straightforward. Yet most of us dread delivering it—so much so that we often put up with poor performance for weeks, months—occasionally perpetually.

Why is it so difficult to fire someone?

Perhaps because we worry about how the employee will react. Will he be emotional? Want to argue? Become aggressive?

Probably it's also because we realize being fired is traumatic—a major blow to self-esteem. The rejection of a firing stings for years; the employee rarely forgets the circumstances, and often remembers the exact words his manager used.

Performing poorly in one job doesn't mean a person is worthless, unemployable, or malevolent. Often, he's simply in the wrong job, isn't ready to work, is distracted by personal issues, or lacks a needed skill. A fired employee almost always eventually finds work he can do.

We can minimize his demoralization and encourage him to find a productive role in society by choosing our words carefully. Being kind, understanding, and respectful is basic human compassion, and in this situation, can make a huge difference, not just in a day, but in a life.

However, being compassionate doesn't mean procrastinating. We have an obligation to maintain a capable and effective team and we should make the change as soon as we determine the person is not appropriate. Putting it off only frustrates our teams and makes it more expensive for our organizations. It also delays the employee in his search for more satisfying work.

Large companies and organizations sometimes have an HR department as well as policies and documents pertaining to terminations. If so, we should notify the HR department, see what's required, and get their input and assistance in planning the termination.

Terminations aren't difficult when we've communicated regularly with the employee and given them open and honest feedback. If they're aware they're doing poorly, they have an opportunity to either improve their performance, or, if they prefer, find other work. Employees who know how they're doing rarely have to be fired.

If we have to initiate the separation, the conversation should be short and respectful.

Firing for Underperformance

Dan has been with ABC several months. Mike and Dan have had several performance conversations, so Dan knows he isn't meeting expectations. Five minutes before quitting time Mike asks Dan to his office.

M: Dan, you're a talented guy but it just hasn't worked out.
D: I was afraid it was coming to that.

M: I'm sorry, Dan. I hope you'll be able to find a spot where you can really use your talents and excel.

Mike doesn't rehash Dan's shortcomings or elaborate on the reasons for termination. That would only demoralize Dan and create hard feelings. The decision has been made, and Mike makes the separation short and blameless.

D: I knew it was coming but I'm not looking forward to telling my family and friends I was fired.
M: I understand. If you'd like, I can allow you to resign. We can honestly say we tried it and mutually agreed that this job wasn't the right fit.
D: That sounds better.

Mike believes allowing an employee to resign is better for both the employee and the company. Firing is poor community relations for the company, and employees don't want a firing on their record. Mike allows Dan to exit with as much dignity and as little damage to his pride as possible.

M: I've asked payroll to continue your pay for three weeks.
D: Thank you. I'll need that.

Mike shares responsibility for the hiring mistake and arranges some assistance to Dan in what is one of life's most difficult times.

M: I'd like to stay friends and keep up with how you're doing. And I'm sure your friends here would enjoy seeing you periodically.

D: What will you tell them about this?

M: Only that you and I discussed it, agreed that the job is probably not the right fit, and you've resigned to look for something else. They're your friends and I believe they'll understand and wish the best for you.

D: It would be nice to stay friends.

Mike prefers to accumulate friends and not enemies. We live in the same community with previous employees, often all our lives.

M: I'll help you gather your things.

Mike keeps the conversation short and avoids discussion of details and reasons as they would serve no useful purpose.

Terminations are less stressful when done at the end of a work day, after most others have left. It's embarrassing for a fired employee to walk through an active work area, gather personal items, and say goodbye to friends, especially if he's visibly emotional.

The situation is uncomfortable for coworkers, too, who, although typically aware of the need for termination (and wondering what took us so long), still feel sympathy for their fired coworker.

Firing someone suddenly, or when we haven't provided continuous performance feedback, is more difficult. The employee is sometimes surprised to hear his performance was unsatisfactory, upset that he wasn't given a chance to improve, and angry at being fired without warning. (Termination lawsuits are often due more to poor communication than to impropriety.)

Firing an Employee Who Doesn't Expect It

*Ed has had multiple confrontations with coworkers, including
a large one this week that has made the work environment stressful.
Since Ed will be surprised, Mike arranges for Tom to stand by.
Just before quitting time Mike asks Ed to come to his office.*

M: Ed, I'm sorry but it just isn't working out for you here.
E: What do you mean it isn't working out?
M: You don't seem happy here, Ed, and your confrontations with your coworkers are creating a difficult environment. We need to part company.

Because Mike hasn't discussed this problem with Ed previously, he offers the reason—but concisely. He doesn't offer or argue the specifics since it wouldn't solve anything, would likely escalate emotions, and might create legal problems.

In employment-at-will areas, no explanation for firing is necessary—a company can simply choose to stop employing a worker. In areas that require a reason for termination, it should be stated as concisely and as non-confrontationally as possible.

E: You're firing me?! Where does that come from?! That's bulls--t! You've got no reason to fire me! None of those arguments were my fault!
M: I'm sorry, Ed. I hope you'll be able to find a job you'll enjoy and excel in.
E: You can't hold it against me that I told Amy she wasn't doing her job! She wasn't! And when they don't do their work, I can't do mine. I can

tell you that nobody could do that job by himself! There should be three people doing it.

M: **I know it's a big job.**

Mike is patient but careful to avoid a debate.

E: Why are you singling me out?! Haley comes in late every other day, Ann calls in sick at least once a week, and Will doesn't know what he's doing.

M: **I'm sorry that this has taken you by surprise, Ed.**

E: Why me?! I just can't accept this. It's not right!

M: **I understand you're upset.**

Mike is correct—Ed is angry because he didn't expect it. Being fired unexpectedly is traumatic and sure to raise emotions; Ed isn't likely to settle down quickly.

E: You're damn right I'm upset. I've got bills to pay and a family to support.

M: **I understand. I've arranged a severance package for you.**

E: [Sarcastically] Thanks a lot.

M: **I'm sorry, Ed. Tom and I will help you gather your things.**

Obviously, firing is much easier when we've been communicating regularly and the employee knows how they're doing. It gives them a chance to improve or find more appropriate work, often avoiding the need for firing altogether.

Terminations should always be immediate and concluded by walking the employee out. Allowing an employee to work the rest of a day, to the end of a payroll period, or any other time only stirs up sympathies and hard feelings. A fired employee isn't likely to get much work done, and hurt feelings might cause him to "even scores" or sabotage work.

If we suspect the employee might get angry, we should have an able-bodied co-worker close by to discourage violence or threats.

If we're voluntarily offering severance pay or any other benefit that isn't required, we can ask the employee to sign a termination agreement stating that he agrees not to initiate or take part in any action against us or the company for improper termination, discrimination, harassment, or other causes.

Some managers like to pay outstanding payroll, vacations, severance, and all further benefits at the time of termination so the employee doesn't worry about whether he'll get it. However, leaving these on the established schedule buys some time for an upset employee to cool down and helps avert any revenge he might initially contemplate.

An employee who commits a serious infraction (fraud, theft, destruction of property, threats, violence, etc.) often must be fired suddenly and unexpectedly.

Once again, the conversation should be short and respectful, and someone should be available to dissuade a violent reaction.

Firing for a Serious Infraction

Paul has been caught for the second time cheating on his timesheet. Mike asks Tom to stand by and invites Paul to his office.

M: Paul, I'm sorry this situation has come up again.

P: I know this looks bad, Mike. I'm sorry. I don't know what I was thinking.

M: You've been a good employee, Paul. I'm very sad that this has hap-
    pened, especially since it doesn't allow me any latitude. I've got no
    choice but to let you go.

P: You mean you're firing me?!

M: I'm sorry, Paul, but I don't have any other options.

It's sometimes tempting, and maybe even seems appropriate, to scold or rebuke a person who stole or intended harm.
But expressing anger or frustration adds nothing useful to an
already emotional situation.

People make mistakes in their lives. Being fired has
many repercussions and is a significant price to pay. We don't
need to pile on.

P: But I've been here four years and I'm one of the best producers you
    have.

M: Yes, you are. And I consider you a friend too. It really hurts me—and
    it's going to hurt the team.

P: Wow! I can't believe you're doing this.

M: I understand this is a shock to you. It is to me too. But you're a smart
    guy and I'm optimistic you'll land on your feet.

P: Is there anything I can say to make you change your mind? I really like
    my job.

M: It would be nice if we could go back and change the circumstances.
    But unfortunately, it's not possible.

P: So, you've made up your mind?

M: Tom and I will help you get your things.

As soon as a termination meeting is over, we should
write a detailed summary for our files that includes the date,
the reason for termination, specific examples illustrating the

reason, a synopsis of the conversation, any promises we made to the employee, and the employee's responses and attitude.

Firing is an uncomfortable responsibility for almost all managers, probably because we sense the consequences for the employee are often traumatic. Although we can't, in fairness to our organizations and our teams, keep people on our teams who aren't performing adequately, we can treat them with consideration, sympathy, and respect. It's our obligation, not just as managers, but as fellow human beings.

Chapter 18

Helping Them Outgrow Us

We could build some amazing teams, get extraordinary results, and save ourselves a lot of time and trouble if our good people stayed in their jobs forever. Every team member would have years of experience and be experts in their responsibilities. We wouldn't have to hire replacements, bring them up to speed, absorb their mistakes, and replace our occasional mishires.

But that's not what our people need. They need to grow in their abilities, responsibilities, impact, and value. They want to progress in their careers, increase their earnings, and provide for their families.

Unselfishly helping our team members advance, outgrow us, and reach their personal goals is perhaps the pinnacle of great management. And, as managers, we're in an ideal position to do it.

Does it seem counterproductive to help our good people advance and leave us?

We do indeed lose some—often our most talented and ambitious. But most of these would leave us anyway. Hopefully the growth and education we provide encourages them to stay a little longer and allows them to contribute more while they're with us.

Others may enjoy and appreciate the supportive environment and decide to stay with the company and manager they've come to trust.

Perhaps even more importantly, creating a growth environment gives us our workplace reputation—something becoming ever more prominent and influential in recruiting. Companies and managers that treat their people with respect and encourage growth and advancement attract high quality team members—an essential element of success.

The ideal opportunity for helping our team members grow is during one-on-ones. If we've created rapport and trust, team members should willingly share their goals with us and welcome our help and encouragement.

M: What would you like to be doing in a few years?

Some may say they like their jobs and are content to stay in them. Perhaps they enjoy the work, like being a respected specialist, are simply comfortable in their surroundings, or have outside interests that the current job allows them to pursue. Climbing the corporate ladder isn't for everyone.

Those who do their jobs well and want to stay put are treasures—they learn their skills thoroughly, minimize mistakes, provide stability, and save us lots of rehiring and retraining. Retention is the greatest bargain in employment.

Learning their preferences allows us to find roles and opportunities they'll enjoy and that can increase their skills, job satisfaction, and earnings.

Others may tell us they haven't settled on a long-term goal. We can often kickstart their thought process.

M: **I've noticed you're good with.... Have you thought about...?**

Some show skills that indicate potential for types of work. Many psychologists and managers feel personality tests are useful in pointing out natural inclinations and abilities.

Occasionally one aspires to unlikely goals.

H: I'd really like to.... [make the pro tour, build a hotel empire, be a movie star, write a best-selling novel, etc.].

Our role doesn't include crushing dreams, no matter how far-fetched. Someone will reach those goals—someone with unwavering belief, self-confidence, energy, and perhaps enough naiveté to ignore the odds. Our petty realism shouldn't deprive the world of great contributions.

But it doesn't hurt them to consider other options in case their plan fails.

M: **Sounds like an ambitious goal; I hope you can make it. Do you think it's a good idea to have a backup plan?**

Many people do aspire to reasonable goals beyond their present jobs. When they share those goals with us, we can often help.

G: I'd like to.... [become an accountant, open a store, become an engineer, teach in college, move up in management]

> M: I think you could be good at that. I enjoy having you on our team, but I'd also like you to reach your goals. How can I help you get there?

Often, we know something about the field or can introduce them to people who can offer details about the work and the paths to it. Occasionally, we can find them a mentor to encourage and guide them through the steps.

When their goal is to advance within our organization or in similar work, we can be especially helpful by offering training, experience, advice, mentorship, and opportunities.

Providing a steady stream of books, videos, manuals, and seminars both educates and helps keep motivation high.

Delegating related responsibilities to them creates experience, builds confidence, and helps them confirm their ambition. We can always find responsibilities to delegate to eager, energetic, and ambitious team members; our list of tasks and potential improvements is typically inexhaustible.

> M: I didn't realize you're an aspiring writer. Would you like to write our weekly meeting summaries? And we need to refine our operating manuals. Is that something you'd be interested in?

Acknowledging their abilities and expertise encourages study and improvement, both to live up to their reputation and to achieve their dreams.

> M: Frank, you're our in-house expert on.... [software, accounting procedure, social media, current styles, etc.] Can we get your opinion on this?

We can, and always should, give generous public credit for their accomplishments, especially to upper management. It's not only the right thing to do, it reflects well on our teams (and on us).

M: Mr. Ryan, did you see Ben's new design? He's created a lot of impressive products for us, and I think this one's another winner.

Some goals require formal education. Tuition assistance is an extraordinary (and unfortunately expensive) job benefit; when it's offered, we should encourage our people to use it (wisely). Sometimes we can offer to accommodate class schedules.

If we or someone on our team knows about schools or other educational options, we can often provide guidance.

But, sometimes the greatest assistance we can offer is just encouragement and help in maintaining their focus.

M: Have you made progress toward your goal since our last conversation? What are your next steps? Have you thought about...? Is there anything I can do to help?

If a team member is applying elsewhere and asks us to be a reference or provide a letter of recommendation, we should do so whole-heartedly, honestly pointing out all his skills and qualities.

And when the time comes for a team member to leave us and pursue their dreams, we can provide a celebratory send-off. We should acknowledge their contribution to the team, encourage them to come back and visit, and, if appropriate, tell them they'd be welcome back to work.

A farewell gift or picture signed by the whole team can evoke positive feelings for a lifetime. And a personal letter from us attesting to their abilities, accomplishments, and value can be a source of pride to them and their families.

Some will come back to visit, see friends, and relive memories.

Others will come back to work (occasionally in higher management).

And some will come back to thank us for helping them become who they are.

Sharing an idea, teaching a skill, and inspiring confidence are never tiresome; they have the power to change the world.

–Mike Mitchell

A Note from Mike

To: My Fellow Travelers on this Management Adventure

I've enjoyed our visit. We have many things in common, don't we?

If I had one wish for you, it would be that you spend your career in management. There's so much satisfaction in building a team, teaching skills, creating confidence, fostering respect, and forming productive lives that... well, I can't imagine why anyone would want to do anything else.

I think we agree that, in the end, lasting value isn't how many widgets we create, how high we climb on the corporate ladder, or how much money we make. It's how we influence the lives we touch. Long after the widgets are worn out, we've retired from our work, and our money is spent, our influence remains. Who can say how far it reaches and how many lives it touches?

And, if any we've managed choose to become managers too, well... I hope it's because they saw in us the joy we got working with them.

If you ever want to talk, have a suggestion, or can correct me in one of my errors, I'd love to hear from you. Please email me at Mike.Mitchell@abbpress.com. (Will you be surprised if I answer you?)

I wish you always the best of teams.

Mike

I'm honored that you've gotten this far in the book and hope you've found something useful.

If there's an idea you'd like to share, something you disagree with, or a situation you'd like to discuss, please email me at *chip.averwater@gmail.com*. I'll answer you—and might include your thoughts in the updates of this book.

And if you enjoyed this book, I'd be grateful if you'd post an honest review on amazon.com or your favorite book website. I read every review and value your feedback. Even a line or two is much appreciated.

Thanks again for reading.

Wishing you great management,

Chip

About the Author

Chip Averwater is retired chairman of Amro Music Stores in Memphis and author of Retail Truths: The Unconventional Wisdom of Retailing.

He and his wife live in Lakeland, TN, outside of Memphis.

Chip enjoys speaking on management, especially outside the U.S., and has been a featured speaker in Europe, Asia, and Australia.

He can be reached at chip.averwater@gmail.com.